VENEZUELA'S EXTERNAL PUBLIC DEBT: LEGAL CONSIDERATIONS FOR ITS RESTRUCTURING

Academy of Political and Social Sciences

RAFAEL BADELL MADRID

VENEZUELA'S EXTERNAL PUBLIC DEBT: LEGAL CONSIDERATIONS FOR ITS RESTRUCTURING

Studies Series
Nº 161

editorial jurídica venezolana international
2026

B141

Badell Madrid, Rafael

Venezuela's external public debt: legal considerations for its restructuring / Rafael Badell Madrid. -- Caracas: Academy of Political and Social Sciences, 2026.
100 p.
Studies Series, 161

ISBN: 978-980-18-7944-2
Legal deposit: DC2026000111

1. EXTERNAL PUBLIC DEBT 2. NATIONAL ECONOMY 3. FINANCIAL NEGOTIATION I. Title

Legal Deposit: DC2026000111

ISBN: 978-980-18-7944-2

Cover: Evelyn Barboza
Layout: Oralia Hernández

Printed in Venezuela

TABLE OF CONTENTS

INTRODUCTION

It should be stated from the outset that a comprehensive restructuring of Venezuela's external public debt is an unavoidable prerequisite for the country's economic and institutional reconstruction in the short to medium term. Therefore, it is necessary to promote a national debate on this issue, which requires urgent planning, as at least four reasons justify its immediacy: (i) Venezuela faces a sovereign debt crisis of extraordinary and unprecedented proportions on the international stage; (ii) the debt's magnitude represents a considerable burden on the eventual recovery of the country's economy; (iii) time is running out, as creditors' pressure for certainty regarding their investments will increase significantly as expectations for the Venezuelan economy become more favorable; and (iv) postponing the necessary measures to safeguard the national patrimony will directly impact the Venezuelan population.

Although this issue might be perceived as secondary to more pressing national challenges, we believe it would be careless to neglect the necessary preparations to navigate this delicate financial situation that jeopardizes the country's economic future. On this basis, the pursuit of sustainable strategies for a comprehensive restructuring should constitute a priority for professionals across disciplines who can contribute proposals aimed at protecting the national patrimony. Contributing in a timely manner to the debate of ideas and proposals is the reason that has motivated this work.

I. EXTERNAL PUBLIC DEBT IN VENEZUELA

For most Venezuelans, *external debt* is a familiar term. It was part of everyday vocabulary throughout the 20th century and a constant feature of the country's economic life, even though its true magnitude and consequences remained largely unknown to the general population. From 2000 onward, the public relevance of external debt began to diminish, both due to the intense political dynamism experienced in the country, and the progressive decline of the national economy, which shifted public attention away from macroeconomic phenomena and toward what has been called a *survival economy*, a reality that has marked the lives of Venezuelans in the last two decades.

1.1. Background

The historical overview of the debt will reveal its continued relevance and assist in contextualizing the current situation. Its usefulness lies in two practical premises: understanding that the issue of external debt is not circumstantial or incidental, but *structural* and has been present throughout our republican history; and remembering that in the face of perhaps more complex credit scenarios, Venezuela was able to recover its international financial credibility by using sensible, yet creative restructuring approaches based on sustainable projects.

1.1.1. Debt as an Original Condition

Venezuela was born *in debt*. Much like the other colonies in the American continent,[1] our external indebtedness was an inherent condition. Already by 1817, the independence movement had required international loans, obtained by direct orders of *Bolívar*, from British financial institutions, intended to finance both war materiel and military campaigns.[2]

---

1 All the Spanish colonies that began independence processes assumed existing external public debt, just as happened with the United States of America after its independence: "The *US has had debt since its inception. Our records show that debts incurred during the American Revolutionary War amounted to $75,463,476.52 by January 1, 1791.* Cf.: "The History of the Debt", *TreasuryDirect website* of the American Treasury Department.

2 "The *Gran Colombian negotiations in London were initially led by Luis López Méndez (...). From 1817 (...) he obtained (...) war resources and various supplies"*. *Cf.:* Rodríguez Campos, Manuel, "Internal and External Debt (1810-1930)" in *Dictionary of Venezuelan History,* Volume 2, Ed. FEP, Caracas, 2011.

By 1821, when the *Gran Colombia* was formally established, the considerable external public debt (estimated at £500,000) forced refinancing to consolidate liabilities that, nevertheless, continued to increase during the long liberation campaign.[3]

The debt *restructuring* has not been foreign to us either. In 1822, still within the Gran Colombian union, the first operation of this type was carried out through the issuance of coupon bonds, derived from the loan agreement signed between Colombian Vice President *Zea* and *Herring, Graham & Powles* (£2,000,000),[4] a loan that required refinancing in just two years with *Goldschmidt & Co.* (for £4,750,000).[5] Thus, when Venezuela proclaimed itself a sovereign nation in 1830, it did so assuming a pre-existing liability: 28.5% of the Gran Colombian union's external public debt[6].

1.1.2. 19th Century: Debt and Restructuring

The inherited amount increased significantly during the militaristic governments of the 19th century, prone to foreign borrowing, resulting in an alarming situation even by today's standards: the Venezuelan go-

---

3 Marichal states: "...*Bolívar decided to sound out the London banking community about the possibility of negotiating a long-term loan to settle debts and obtain additional funds for his army. The first Latin American external loan would therefore be a war loan*". *Cf.*: Marichal, Carlos, *Historia de la deuda externa de América Latina: Desde la independencia hasta la gran depresión, 1820-1930*, Alianza Editorial, Mexico, 1988, pp. 17 ff.

4 "*The bonds were sold on the London Stock Exchange at an original price of 80% and were presumably purchased by more than a thousand English investors. The interest* [at 6%] *was to be paid for 27 years every six months in London by the bankers Barclay, Tritton, Bevan & Co....*". *Cf.*: Liehr, Reinhard, "The External Debt of Gran Colombia to Great Britain 1820-1860" in *The public debt in Latin America in historical perspective*, Bibliotheca Ibero-Americana Vervuert, Madrid, 1995, pp 466-488.

5 Rodríguez Campos, *Op. Cit.*, p. 87.

6 Berglund highlights: "*From the very beginning, Venezuela had been paying a portion of the Colombian domestic debt because it was charged against Venezuelan revenues. The British bondholders began pressing for a settlement of the foreign debt as early as 1832, in part because the domestic debt was being paid (a pattern which would be repeated in the future). However, it was made clear to them that any formal discussions would have to wait until Venezuela, Colombia and Ecuador agreed to a division of the debt. Such an agreement was signed in late 1834 but was not ratified by the Colombian Congress until 1837. Under its terms, Venezuela was assigned 28½ percent of both the domestic and the foreign debt of the Republic of Colombia.*" Berglund, Susan, "The Public Debt of Venezuela: Causes and Effects, 1830-1870", in Liehr, Reinhard, *Op. cit.*, p. 421.

vernment carried out nine restructuring processes in a period of barely 60 years (1840-1900). At least three during *Páez's* government (1840, 1848, 1862); five during *Guzmán Blanco*'s governments (1863, 1864, 1872, 1874, 1880), and a consolidation under *Joaquín Crespo*'s government, negotiated with the *Disconto-Gesellschaft* (now *Deutsche Bank)* in 1896.[7] With such background, far from being extraordinary, the restructuring of external debt was *characteristic* of Venezuelan public finances since the origin of the Republic.[8]

1.1.3. Default of 1902

Default is likewise not unprecedented. Of particular significance is the default arising from the unilateral suspension of payments on foreign debt obligations decreed by President *Cipriano Castro* in 1902.[9] This action prompted an international political crisis that climaxed in the blockade of Venezuelan ports by German, British, and Italian vessels[10] exercising a coercive collection of debts under the "*gunboat diplomacy.*"[11]

This situation, largely resolved by President *Roosevelt's* intervention and the signing of the *Washington Protocols* in 1903,[12] had significant repercussions both nationally and internationally. On the one hand, Venezuela experienced the consequences of default in a belligerent environment; on the other, it led to the formulation of two significant diplomatic policies: the *Drago Doctrine,* summarized as abstaining from

7 For information on successive public credit operations, see: Rodríguez Campos, Manuel, *Op. Cit.*, pp 88-90; and in more detail, Pimentel y Roth, Francisco, *Historia del crédito público en Venezuela,* Ministerio de Crédito Público, Caracas, 1974.

8 Pimentel, Francisco, *Chronological summary of the laws and decrees of public credit in Venezuela since the year 1826,* Ministry of Public Credit, Caracas, 1873.

9 "*The scenario that would later generate the conflict with the European powers was presumably determined by Cipriano Castro's intransigent stance in refusing to pay any loans, interest, or reimbursements for damages incurred before May 23, 1899.*" *Cf.*: Salazar, Andrés, and Ospina, Ramón, "The Blockade of the Venezuelan Coast: A Brief Encounter with European Imperialism," *Scientific,* 9(31), 68–86, 2024.

10 Mitchell, Nancy, "Venezuela Blockade (1902-1903)" in Martel, Gordon, *The Encyclopedia of War,* Wiley-Blackwell, 2011.

11 Mandel, Robert, "The Effectiveness of Gunboat Diplomacy", *International Studies Quarterly,* V. 30-1, Oxford University Press, 1986. In Spanish, the expression has been translated as "diplomacy *of the gunboats.*"

12 Rojas Sardi, Armando, *The United States and the 1902 blockade: external debt: aggression of the new times,* National Academy of History, 1992.

the use of force to collect public debt;[13] and the *Calvo Doctrine,* which advocates the preeminence of local jurisdiction over foreign claims.[14] While not considered a principle of public international law per se, the *Calvo Clause* was nonetheless adopted virtually unanimously by Latin American countries and, in the case of Venezuela, incorporated into all constitutional texts from 1893 onward as the *clause of immunity from jurisdiction,* a provision that exist to date in Article 151 of the Constitution of the Bolivarian Republic of Venezuela of 1999 ("CRBV").[15]

The purpose was to prevent Venezuela from being sued abroad for disputes arising from external debt contracts (public loans) deemed to be in the *national interest,*[16] an application that would ultimately prove "relative" (since the exclusion of international lawsuits in Venezuelan external debt contracts is practically the exception rather than the rule.) Nevertheless, the categorization of contracts as being in the national public interest would prove relevant, as we shall see, for the vast majority of the nation's future credit operations.

1.1.4. Extinction of the Debt (1930)

Following the 1903 agreements, the Republic undertook actions aimed at immediately servicing its external debt and eventually set out

13 In response to the international blockade against Venezuela, the Argentine Minister of Foreign Affairs, Dr. Luis María Drago, sent a diplomatic note to Washington in which he stated, among other things, the following: "*The recognition of the debt, the settlement of its amount, can and should be carried out by the nation without prejudice to its fundamental rights as a sovereign entity; but the compulsory and immediate collection, at any given moment, by means of force, would bring nothing but the ruin of the weaker nations and the absorption of their government, with all the powers inherent to it, by the strong of the earth.*" *Cf.*: Fabela, Isidro, *The Monroe and Drago Doctrines,* UNAM, Mexico, 1957.

14 Tamburini, Francesco, "History and destiny of the 'Calvo Doctrine': current relevance or obsolescence of the thought of Carlos Calvo?", *Journal of Historical-Legal Studies,* International Law, Valparaíso, Chile, 2002.

15 CRBV: "Article *151. In contracts of public interest, if it is not inappropriate according to the nature of the same, a clause shall be considered incorporated, even if it is not express, according to which the doubts and controversies that may arise about said contracts and that are not resolved amicably by the contracting parties, shall be decided by the competent courts of the Republic, in accordance with its laws, without giving rise to foreign claims for any reason or cause*".

16 On the subject in general see: Sansó, Beatrice, "Jurisdictional immunity in Article 151 of the 1999 Constitution", in *Homage Book to Enrique Tejera París, Topics on the 1999 Constitution,* Center for Legal Research, Caracas, 2001, pp 333-368.

to pay it off completely,[17] a goal achieved three decades later after remarkable efforts, exemplary economic measures, and long-term fiscal planning. Certainly, one consequence of the *Castro* government being compelled to make urgent payments on interest and principal, was the establishment of a 30% extraordinary tax on imports and customs duties, which effectively increased revenue to ensure the continued servicing of the debt.[18] These measures, together with the oil revenues received from 1914 onward, allowed Venezuela to rapidly increase its reserves, a condition that enabled the *Gómez* administration to cancel the entire external debt in 1930,[19] on the centenary of the *Liberator's* death.[20] Venezuela was thus the only country in Latin America to fully repay its external debt throughout the 20th century.

1.1.5. 20th Century: Cyclical Debt

After its extinction, Venezuela did not incur new foreign financial commitments until the mid-1950s,[21] when the government of *Pérez Jiménez* converted incipient liabilities into a novel *floating debt,* which continued to increase during the governments of *Betancourt, Leoni* and *Caldera,* despite the tripling of the ordinary tax revenues between 1959 and 1973, as a result of oil revenue.

The situation became more complicated from 1974 onward, with the increase in public spending during *Pérez's* first term. Financed by debt backed by crude oil exports, this spending reignited the cycle of indebtedness, quadrupling the existing public debt in just four years.[22] The *Herrera Campíns* administration -a critic of inherited

---

17 Rodríguez Campos, *Op. Cit.*, p. 92.

18 *Idem.*

19 *See:* "Relationship of the Moratoriums and Renegotiations of Latin American Debts between 1931-1950" and the amounts of consolidated debts for 1933: Marichal, Carlos, *Op. Cit.*, p. 156 et seq.

20 "Venezuela *is debt-free and owes nothing to anyone,*" Gómez stated in a national address.

21 The compulsive collection actions "*left a traumatic experience for Venezuela*" and that "*harsh lesson from the beginning of the century remained in force for a long time and was something like a rule of national honor not to resort to external public credit.*" *Cf.*: Maza Zavala, Domingo, "Debt 1935-1993" in *Dictionary of Venezuelan History,* Volume 2, Ed. FEP, p. 95.

22 "*In the period 1974-1978 (...) net public indebtedness increased (...) by 482%, if only authorized debt is taken into account...* ". *Ibid.*, p. 97.

liabilities[23]- contributed to further amplifying the debt through transactions undertaken by the newly formed decentralized entities (State-owned corporations),[24] increasing the figure to US$27 billion by 1984,[25] despite the economic boom experienced between 1979 and 1982.

1.1.6. Restructuring Processes of 1985 and 1990

This situation gave rise to a national discussion regarding the need to restructure external debt to achieve financial stability internationally, which led to two major restructuring processes at the end of the 20th century: one carried out during the first year of the *Lusinchi* administration (1985), as a forced measure imposed by foreign creditor banks that insisted in the supervision of the International Monetary Fund (IMF), a process that culminated in 1987 in a relatively satisfactory manner; and another carried out during the second *Pérez* administration (1989-1990), within the framework of the *Brady Plan* (launched by the United States for the restructuring of near-default Latin American debts), which was carried out through the *1990 Financing Plan.*[26]

1.1.7. 21st Century

External debt remained relatively small, but the restructured sum augmented during *Caldera's second term* (1999), although it reached a somewhat manageable level (US$20 billion) that was maintained until the early years of the *Chávez's* government (1999-2001).[27] For this

---

23 He uttered the famous phrase "*I am receiving a mortgaged Venezuela*" in his inaugural speech before Congress (1979).

24 Kelly, Janet, "State-owned enterprises. From commonplace to common sense" in Naím, Moisés, and Piñango, Ramón, *The Case of Venezuela: an illusion of harmony,* IESA, Caracas, 1985, p. 141.

25 "The *contradiction between the fiscal boom, manifested in the highest ordinary revenues, unprecedented in the history of Venezuelan public finances, and the speed of public indebtedness, without economic or social emergencies being met through the application of resources obtained from credit, is particularly noteworthy". Cf.*: Maza Zavala, *Op. Cit.*, p. 97.

26 On the subject, *see:* Hernández Delfino, Carlos, "Venezuela and the Brady Initiative", *Prodavinci,* Caracas, 2021.

27 According to Alayón and Marcano, between 1999 and 2006, Venezuela's external debt, solely in terms of bonds, remained around US$20 billion. *See*: Alayón, Ángel, "Venezuela: la deuda externa en figuras," *Prodavinci,* Caracas, 2017.

reason, it has been argued that by the beginning of the 21st century, Venezuela's external debt was sustainable and even "payable" without having to resort to extraordinary measures.

1.2. Theoretical Framework of Debt

The concept of *public debt* dates back to the origins of economics and currency,[28] but it has evolved over time as a consequence of the growth of the public administration, as well as the assumption by the State of new and multiple business functions through functionally decentralized administration.[29] For the sake of terminological precision, we will limit ourselves to a brief *conceptual typology* that will aid our discussion, since the limited scope of this analysis prevents us from delving into technical aspects of credit matters, more suitable for an economic study.

1.2.1. Conceptualization of External Debt

The internationally accepted notion of external debt, adopted by multilateral organizations (IMF and World Bank), generally refers to all credit obligations incurred by a country *(public sector)* or its residents *(private sector)* for the payment of principal and/or interest to foreign entities *(financial institutions, creditors, or governments.)*[30] It is a comprehensive and all-encompassing concept that comprises all obligations, both public and private. Although private external debt has also been a determining factor in Venezuela's history, its magnitude has been smaller and, in retrospect, has caused fewer problems;[31] therefore, we take interest herein in the notion of *public* external debt.

---

28 As Graeber highlights: "*... one of the first effects of the arrival of a commercial economy was a series of debt crises, of the sort long familiar from Mesopotamia and Israel.*" Graeber, David, *Debt: The First 5000 Years,* Melville House Publishing, New York, 2011.

29 Maza Zavala, *Op. cit.,* p. 95.

30 International Monetary Fund, IMF Fund, *External Debt Statistics: Guide for Compilers and Users,* 2023; and the World Bank's *Global Development Finance Database.* For Easterly, the concept refers to the set of financial obligations contracted by a country with foreign entities, representing a commitment to repay the principal with interest within a specified period. *See:* Easterly, William, "Debt Relief", *Foreign Policy,* Vol. 127, Nov/Dec 2001.

31 Regarding the problems of payment of private external debt by mid-1980, *see:* Brewer-Carías, Allan R., "The vicissitudes of the payment of private external debt and the legal

1.2.2. Public Debt

Debt represented by all credit obligations assumed by the *Public Sector* with foreign creditors, which includes the Republic and the decentralized territorial entities, the States and Municipalities, as well as the functionally decentralized entities, which are embodied in the autonomous institutes and the state-owned corporations (important actors in the assumption of international credits in Venezuela since the mid-1970s.)[32]

Notwithstanding the distinction made quite briefly herein, ***external public debt***, whether sovereign or assumed by state-owned enterprises, includes all obligations that represent a liability: international loans and subsequent financial operations that entail the issuance of securities (debt bonds and others), whether consolidated net debt or floating debt;[33] and liabilities arising from contractual and extra-contractual obligations, as well as accessory liability for compliance or non-compliance with those obligations -which constitute a debt that is not strictly derived from credit financial operations with respect to its origin- which are not always rigorously computed within the data of total external public debt, as has happened in the case of Venezuela.[34]

---

incongruities of the executive power", *Revista de Derecho Público,* No. 27, Editorial Jurídica Venezolana, pp 36-49, 1986.

32 *See:* Escobar, Gustavo, "The Labyrinth of Economics" in Naím and Piñango, *Op. Cit.*, pp 74-101.

33 From the time of the Spanish Crown (1500-1600), royal financial operations were carried out consisting of short-term loans with interest, called "asientos," which were recorded in the accounting records as *floating debt* and became *consolidated debt* through "juros". *See*: Comín, Francisco, *Las crises de la deuda soberana en España (1500-2015),* Los Libros de la Catarata, Madrid, 2016. However, as Maza points out, in the modern history of Venezuela, floating debt, generally assumed by public companies, quickly became part of the general sovereign debt through refinancing due to default. *See:* Maza Zavala, *Op. Cit.*, p. 95.

34 This has been highlighted by almost all researchers on the subject, who emphasize that debt from loan agreements and bond issuances represents only a fraction of the total debt, which includes all types of liabilities attributable to the public sector, of a very diverse nature. Hernández has indicated that in Venezuela: "the *so-called non-financial debt* [is] a *category that is a kind of catch-all, since it includes very dissimilar securities: contractual breaches, especially with PDVSA contractors; defaults on promissory notes issued by PDVSA; obligations arising from expropriations, confiscations, occupations, and other similar measures; and obligations derived from final judgments and arbitration awards."* Hernández, José Ignacio, *"What is happening with Venezuela's external public debt?"*, article published in *La Gran Aldea,* February 2022.

Hence, within this study, the distinction of the financial *origin* of the debt will be relevant, because although any comprehensive restructuring must address the entire spectrum of existing external public debt, that derived from sovereign bonds or state-owned enterprises -a significant part of the *default*- deserves attention due to its particular regulation.

1.2.3. Sovereign Debt

Debt assumed directly by the Republic or the Nation and governed by a foreign jurisdiction[35] (also referred to in Venezuela as *direct debt.*)[36] Presently, this notion generally suggests the issuance of securities or instruments (*bonds*) in the international market[37].

1.2.4. Financial Debt

a) Origins

The financial mechanism of transforming loans into sovereign bonds has existed since the origins of monarchical debt, and is documented from the mid-1600s, during the reign of Charles II in England, when "*assured treasury orders*" were issued-Crown debt securities subject to the payment of principal and interest, the non-payment of which caused significant problems for the existing financial system.[38]

---

35 "In *international market practice, the term sovereign debt is used to refer to state debt that is implemented through the issuance of bonds traded in public offerings on stock exchanges. The term includes any loan agreement entered into by the Public Administration with a private individual or with an international organization, and which is implemented through the issuance of bonds in different currencies and jurisdictions". Cf.:* Carrasquero, Andrés, Escovar, Ramón, Campos, Mariana, and Freitas, Víctor, *Sovereign Debt Restructuring Processes: Lessons Learned for Venezuela from Uruguay, Greece, Puerto Rico and Argentina,* CEDICE, 2023, p. 6.

36 Maza Zavala, *Op. cit.,* p. 98.

37 Calvo, Guillermo, "Servicing the Public Debt: The Role of Expectations," *The American Economic Review,* Vol. 78, No. 4 (Sep), 1988, pp. 647–661; and Buchheit, Lee, and Gulati, Mitu, "How to Restructure Greek Debt," *Duke Law School Public Law & Legal Theory Series,* May 2010. These types of liabilities are generally issued in international capital markets and governed by foreign laws, which can make their restructuring difficult in the event of default. *See:* Portes, Richard, Freixas, Xavier, and Dewatripont, Mathías, *Macroeconomic Stability and Financial Regulation,* Center for Economic and Policy Research, 2009; and Borensztein, Eduardo, and Panizza, Ugo, *The Costs of Sovereign Debt Default,* IMF Working Paper, International Monetary Fund, 2008.

38 Milevsky, Moshe, *The Day the King Defaulted: Financial Lessons from the Stop of the Exchequer in 1672,* Macmillan, 2017.

In America, by the year 1776, the English colonies had already issued "*loan certificates*" to finance the independence wars;[39] and in Spain, in 1780, at the end of the reign of Charles III, "*royal vouchers*" were introduced, debt securities redeemable after twenty years with a 4% coupon, which had the unique characteristic of being usable as paper money and which, over time, came to be known simply as *national debt securities*,[40] coexisting with the later "*liquidated credit notes.*"[41]

These historical precedents, among others, laid the groundwork for the issuance of debt securities under various names, but with a common essence: *financial instruments, in the form of bonds, designed to allow nations to obtain loans and extraordinary resources.* This practice, which began in the monarchies of the 16th century, gradually became a fundamental tool for financing projects and managing national economies.

Currently, public credit operations in the international arena generally take this form: international credits or loans that force nations to resort to the issuance of bonds, whether sovereign or belonging to the public sector in general, with or without a coupon, guaranteed or not, but generally governed by foreign regulations, insofar as they are generally traded in international markets.

It is important to clarify that public debt terminology does not explicitly classify these types of issuances as "financial *debt*"; it is a rather informal term that has practical usefulness based on the distinction between the origin of the debt: debt derived from financial instruments *versus* debt arising from other types of international commitments. On the one hand, bond regulations involve a complexity (generally international rules and special conditions) that often exceeds that of conventional bilateral loans; on the other hand, they involve an indeterminate number of creditors with varying credit ratings and interests, presenting challenges distinct from those encountered in negotiations of bilateral or non-contractual obligations.

39 "The History of the Debt", American Department of the Treasury, *TreasuryDirect website.*

40 Comín, Francisco, *Op. Cit.*

41 It is worth noting that almost all of those original sovereign bonds fell into *default,* suspension, or other circumstances that led to the need for their restructuring.

b) Debt derived from financial instruments in Venezuela

For purposes of this work, we will hereinbelow refer to debt *arising from financial operations* as public debt bond issuances, whether sovereign or issued by decentralized public administrations.[42] Under this definition, we will refer to bonds requiring restructuring due to the recent *default*.

(i) Sovereign bonds issued as direct, unconditional, unsecured and general obligations, maturing between 2018 and 2038 ("Sovereign *Bonds*"); and

(ii) Bonds issued by the state-owned company *Petróleos de Venezuela S.A.* (PDVSA), under different conditions, such as direct, unconditional obligations with or without guarantee, maturing between 2017 and 2037 ("PDVSA *Bonds*").[43]

(iii) Although there are also bonds from other public companies (i.e.: Elecar, Sidetur, Corpoelec),[44] for the purposes of this study they will be grouped under the same category as PDVSA.

Particular interest in the legal actions stemming from the *default* lies with the *PDVSA 2020 Bonds*. These bonds resulted from a

---

[42] State-owned corporations were major players in the accumulation of debt from the mid-1970s onward, and their liabilities were often eventually consolidated as sovereign debt by the Republic. As Kelly pointed out: "*...the external debt of public enterprises had come to constitute more than 70 percent of the public debt by the end of 1982. [...] The data (...) show that public enterprises have jeopardized the financial stability of the State with this excessive contracting of foreign loans. [...] With the collaboration of foreign banks, the companies contracted loans higher than their own capacity to repay allowed, which was unequivocally revealed when the oil market contracted in 1982". See:* Kelly, Janet, *Op. Cit.*, p. 141.

[43] "*These are 25 bond issues made between 1997 and 2016. All of these bonds are in default. In the case of seven bonds [Elecar 2018, Venezuela 2018 (US922646AT10), Venezuela 2018 (US922646BE32), Venezuela 2018 (USP97475AD26), Venezuela 2019 (USP97475AN08), PDVSA 2020 (USP7807HAV70) and Venezuela 2020 (USP97475AG56)], the default is due to the failure to pay the principal after the maturity date; as for the rest of the bonds, it is due to the failure to pay interest since the end of 2017." Cf.*: Carrasquero, Andrés, Escovar, Ramón, and Campos, Mariana, *Venezuelan External Debt derived from Bonds*, CEDICE, 2022.

[44] Bonds issued by CA La Electricidad de Caracas (Elecar), a company controlled by PDVSA at the time of issuance; by the National Electric Corporation, SA (Corpoelec); as well as by Siderúrgica del Turbio, SA (Sidetur).

2016-2017 exchange of unsecured bonds, leading to a new issuance secured by collateral (50.1% of *PDV Holdings' shares)* held by the American company *Citgo Holdings,*[45] which owns all shares of *Citgo Petroleum Company,* the holder of Venezuelan oil assets abroad.[46] The consequences of this particular issuance,[47] as well as the pending legal actions, will be crucial to the restructuring process.

1.3. Legal Nature of External Public Debt

In Venezuelan law, all external public debt operations carried out by the public sector are classified as *public credit operations.* Since these operations are generally contractual commitments with foreign entities, they may also be exceptionally classified as *contracts of national public interest.*

1.3.1. Public Credit Operation

Public credit refers to debt operations issued by public entities or traded in public markets. Generally speaking, the concept of *public credit* refers to the capacity of public entities to obtain economic resources to cover public expenditures through financing operations. Historically, this capacity was based on their "political, *economic, legal, and moral aptitude (...) based on the trust they enjoy due to their assets (...) and their conduct.*"[48]

---

45 As is known, Citgo was a long-established private oil company, founded in 1910 as the *Cities Service Company* and acquired mostly by PDVSA in 1986 (fully in 1990), along with all its assets, such as the Corpus Christi refinery in Texas (https://www.citgo.com/about/our-history).

46 In addition to the publicly available information on this discussed matter, *see:* Badell Madrid, Rafael, "Comments on Judgment No. 821 of the Political-Administrative Chamber of the Supreme Tribunal of Justice dated December 8, 2022, referring to contracts of national public interest", in *Revista de Derecho Público No. 171-172,* Editorial Jurídica Venezolana, Caracas, 2022, p. 319.

47 *See*: Duque Corredor, Román, "Nullity of the PDVSA 2020 Bonds" in *Revista de Derecho Público,* No. 161-162, Editorial Jurídica Venezolana, Caracas, 2022, pp. 349-352; Pellegrino, Cosimina and Louza, Laura, "PDVSA signed a contract of national public interest without even the endorsement of the National Assembly" in *Revista de Derecho Público,* No. 171-172, Editorial Jurídica Venezolana, Caracas, 2022, p. 111; and Brewer-Carías, Allan R., "The failed attempt by the National Assembly to exercise political control over the public administration by investigating the actions of PDVSA, and its annulment by the Constitutional Chamber" in *Revista de Derecho Público,* No. 147-148, Editorial Jurídica Venezolana, Caracas, 2016, p. 359.

48 Oría, Salvador, *Finance,* Buenos Aires, 1948.

Thus, it is one of the common techniques to obtain resources for *extraordinary expenses:* while ordinary expenses are covered by revenues provided for in the legal system, either by legal mandate (e.g.: revenues from the constitutional allocation) or through the exercise of the administrative entity's own powers (i.e. tax revenues),[49] extraordinary expenses arise from short- or medium-term needs of an exceptional nature that cannot be met with the resources authorized for ordinary expenses. However, at least in Venezuelan practice, we have observed that the use of public credit has not necessarily occurred due to the need to generate "extraordinary resources, but also through routine administrative actions that involve a commitment of public assets. Therefore, the legislator has come to consider these as public debts as well, subject to the same control mechanisms as extraordinary operations.

In any case, public credit operations, which constitute the common means by which public entities obtain *short-term resources,* derive from debt mechanisms or, at least, from the commitment of public assets, and, therefore, must be provided for within the constitutional framework and shall be legally expanded. Since 1826, Venezuela has had extensive legislation regarding public credit, given that *loans* constituted one of the main forms of financing from the formation of the Republic until well into the 20th century.[50]

However, this study shall be limited to citing the current basis for public credit operations, the main one being external public debt derived from *financial operations,* which is provided for in article 312 of the CRBV:

> "The *law will set limits on public debt in accordance with a prudent level in relation to the size of the economy, productive investment, and the capacity to generate revenue to cover public debt service. Public credit operations will require, for their validity, a special law authorizing them, except for the exceptions established by the organic law. The special law will indicate the moda-*

---

[49] On the subject, *see:* Brewer-Carías, Allan R., "Public Power" in *Political and Constitutional Institutions,* Volume II, pp. 144.

[50] Pimentel y Roth, Francisco, *History of public credit in Venezuela,* General Archive of the Nation, 1974.

lities of the operations and authorize the corresponding budget appropriations in the respective budget law."
The special law on annual indebtedness will be presented to the National Assembly together with the Budget Law.
The State shall not recognize any obligations other than those contracted by legitimate organs of the National Power, in accordance with the law."

The drafters of the constitution delegated to the legislature the power to set *limits on public debt* according to a "prudent" level in relation to the economy and, above all, *the capacity to generate revenue* to cover debt service-a warning that has frequently been underestimated and has consequently led to debt restructurings. In any case, the aforementioned provision refers to two legal mandates: the special law on annual borrowing, and the organic law that will establish and regulate these operations.

It was precisely in execution of this provision that the aforementioned Organic Law of Public Administration ("LOAF") was enacted in 2000, with the purpose of regulating in a single text the aspects previously contained in various laws (i.e.: budgetary, public debt, and national treasury),[51] as well as organizing the *public credit system,* previously established in successive public credit laws.[52] The LOAF includes various regulations to develop the budgetary, treasury, and other systems, but we will focus hereafter on the rules contained in Regulation No. 2 of the LOAF, mentioned above, which developed the *Public Credit System* and expanded upon the technical aspects contained in the Law.

---

51 Its latest reform was published in Official Gazette No. 6,210 Extraordinary of December 30, 2016.

52 "According *to the Statement of Reasons, the drafting of this law responds to the need to adapt the regulations governing fiscal processes to the requirements of the new Constitution, whose innovation in fiscal matters focuses almost exclusively on the issue of macro-fiscal rules. In this sense, it proposes subjecting fiscal management to the principles of efficiency, solvency, transparency, responsibility, and fiscal balance, for which it establishes the obligation to limit public spending and debt, the creation of a macroeconomic stabilization fund, the intertemporal distribution of subsoil wealth, the explicit formulation of long-term fiscal policy, fiscal balance and sustainability, the coordination of macroeconomic policies, and fiscal responsibility". See:* Moreno, María Antonia, "The Organic Law of Public Sector Financial Administration. Content, Scope, and Limitations" in *Venezuelan Journal of Current Affairs Analysis,* Vol. VII-2, UCV, Caracas, 2001.

The LOAF defined public credit as "the *capacity of the entities governed by this Law to incur debt*" and stipulated that such entities would be the Republic, the States, and the Municipalities, as well as other legal entities under public law, a comprehensive term that also includes functionally decentralized entities (autonomous institutes, state-owned corporations, as well as foundations, civil associations, and other institutions established with public funds) (Art. 6). Furthermore, it expressly defined what would be considered *public credit* operations and included within these all-debt operations (contracting loans, *issuing and placing securities,* including treasury bills).

1.3.2. Exceptional category: Contract of National Public Interest

Once the general principle has been established, it is appropriate to refer to a special type of public credit operations that may exceptionally also constitute *contracts of national public interest.*

It is important to clarify beforehand that public credit operations are generally carried out through conventional mechanisms (*contracts*) which, because they directly involve the Administration (*public sector*) and the public interest, are *administrative contracts in nature.* Within these contracts, some may be classified as being of *national interest* or of *national public interest,* which refers to an indeterminate and widely discussed notion in Venezuelan doctrine. By way of consensus and based on jurisprudential criteria, we will summarize it as referring to contracts entered into by the Republic, through the competent bodies of the National Executive, as well as by the States and Municipalities, whose object is *essential for the purposes of the State* and whose *amount* may affect *national economic interests* or involve payment over several fiscal years.[53]

[53] The Venezuelan doctrinal discussion on this matter has been extensive and includes various positions of interest: Farías Mata, Lares Martínez, Brewer-Carías, Melich-Orsini, Caballero Ortíz, Ramos Martínez, and others-which merit a separate analysis that cannot be developed in depth in this work, which presents the binding criterion of the decision of the Constitutional Chamber of the Supreme Tribunal of Justice of September 24, 2002 (Case: *Andrés Velásquez, Elías Mata, and others).* Thus, for the purposes of this study, we will limit ourselves to highlighting that there are debt operations that will be considered *contracts of national public interest* and, in particular, restructuring has received this juris-

The origin of this conceptualization stemmed from the inclusion of this classification of contracts in the constitutional clause of immunity from jurisdiction, now provided for in Article 151 of the CRBV, whose origin is found in the Constitution of 1864 (Art. 72, Ord. 8°) which attributed to the *President of the Union* the power to enter into this type of contract and submit it to the legislature, a provision that remained unchanged in the constitutions of 1874, 1881, 1891 and 1893 (which already made reference to the President of the Republic and to the authorization of Congress), to be included in similar terms in the constitutional texts of 1901, 1904, 1909, 1914, 1922, 1925 (reference to contracts of railway lines, aerial cables, telegraphic communications, immigration), 1928, 1929, 1931 and 1936, until 1947, where the notions of contracts of national interest and contracts of public interest were merged, which was maintained in the Constitution of 1961 and 1999, without expressly defining that category.

Therefore, from its inception, this classification required determining the type of contract/transaction through a *case-by-case examination,* and generally, not only large-scale contracts were considered as such, but also those entered into between the nation and foreign entities, given that these gave rise to claims outside the country.[54] For our study, the importance of analyzing this special nature of contracts and their conceptualization stems from two reasons:

a) On the one hand, because certain typical public credit operations may exceptionally be classified as *contracts of national public interest* due to their nature or magnitude, and this must be analyzed on a case-by-case basis; and
b) On the other hand, because with respect to the *refinancing operations* of public debt with foreign entities (external debt), all of them were expressly considered as part of that special

---

prudential classification from the Supreme Tribunal of Justice. On this topic, see in general the studies: Badell Madrid, Rafael, "Contracts *of National Public Interest,*" in *Revista de Derecho Administrativo,* No. 19, July-December 2004, Caracas, 2004; Badell Madrid, Rafael, "Contracts of Public Interest" in *Public Law Review,* No. 159-160, Venezuelan Legal Publishing House, Caracas, 2021. It is worth noting, as a corollary, that the Constitutional Chamber subsequently excluded from this classification the contracts entered into by PDVSA, as we shall see.

54 Toro Jiménez, Fermín, *Manual of Public International Law,* Caracas, 1982, pp. 481 et seq.

category of contracts by the Constitutional Chamber of the Supreme Tribunal of Justice in a binding interpretation of articles 150 and 151 of the CRBV.[55]

This, to some extent, resolves the debate regarding the legal nature of refinancing and restructuring operations and makes it unnecessary to determine, on a case-by-case basis, whether a particular process meets the doctrinal and jurisprudential conditions to be considered of national public interest. However, this circumstance requires us to study the requirements and procedures that apply to this type of contract in order to initiate external public debt restructuring processes, which is the scenario at hand.

Before concluding this section, it is essential for this study to highlight a controversial issue related to the decision of the Constitutional Chamber of the Supreme Tribunal of Justice, in ruling No. 2,241 of September 3, 2000 (case: *Annulment of Article 809 of the Organic Law of the Financial Administration*), which excluded agreements signed by PDVSA from being classified as *contracts of national public interest,* restricting that notion to contracts signed by territorial entities (the Republic, States, and Municipalities). This decision, widely discussed by acknowledged authorities,[56] expressly sought to ensure that even contracts of significant economic magnitude or essential to the nation's objectives would not be considered of national public interest and, therefore, would not be subject to parliamentary authorization by the National Assembly. Without going into the possible discussions that this

---

[55] In the same decision cited, the Constitutional Chamber stated: "*...there are other public credit operations that do generate contracts of national public interest, and therefore, of mandatory prior control by the National Assembly, such as those operations in which the loan of resources is agreed upon, with the consequent indebtedness for the Nation, or the refinancing of the external public debt is agreed upon, among others".*

[56] In particular, Brewer-Carías indicated that he does not share this view, stating: "Therefore, *according to the Supreme Tribunal's doctrine on Article 150 of the 1999 Constitution, a contract signed, for example, by Petróleos de Venezuela (PDVSA) could not be considered a contract of national public interest, which makes no sense. However, it is undoubtedly a national public contract signed by a state-owned public entity, specifically a state-owned enterprise or a state-owned private legal entity". Cf.*: Brewer-Carías, Allan R., "New Considerations on the Legal Regime of State Contracts in Venezuela" in *Revista de Derecho Administrativo,* No. 2, Caracas, 2006.

raised, it serves to understand that the aim has been to exclude the state oil company from parliamentary control, weakening the authorization procedure that the constituent assembly sought in Venezuela since the mid-19th century.

1.4. Internal Procedure for the Assumption of External Public Debt

Since all public debt transactions constitute public credit, we will briefly refer to the general procedure and requirements for debt transactions stipulated in the LOAF that have this classification. In general, all transactions of this nature begin through an administrative procedure that complies with the following steps:

(i) *Special Law:* The general principle is that all public credit operations require authorization by means of a special law issued by the National Assembly for that purpose, which is specified in the *Special Law on Indebtedness.* This law must stipulate in its text the internal and external public debt operations that the National Executive may carry out in each fiscal year (Art. 79). However, as we will see, this will not apply to restructurings or refinancings that seek to *improve* the conditions of public debt (Art. 100).[57]

(ii) *Ministry of Finance:* Taking as a legal basis that legislative authorization for indebtedness, the *National Office of Public Credit,* in coordination with the Vice Minister of Financial Management, will formally request the Minister of Finance to initiate an internal procedure for each public debt operation (art. 16, RLOAF No. 2).

(iii) *National Executive:* the operation will consist of a request submitted by the Minister of Finance for approval by the President of the Republic in the Council of Ministers (art. 17, RLOAF No. 2).

---

[57] Restructurings or refinancings are exempt from the requirement of authorization by Special Law, provided that they aim to improve debt conditions, reduce the agreed interest rate, extend the payment term, convert external debt into internal debt, reduce cash flow, or allow for savings in financing costs (Art. 100, LOAF). However, some refinancing operations may not have these objectives, and in such cases, they must be authorized by Special Law, as stipulated in Article 59 of Regulation No. 2 of the LOAF.

(iv) *Central Bank of Venezuela (BCV):* Once the operation is approved by the National Executive, the technical opinion of the BCV is required on "*the monetary impact and financial conditions of each public credit operation*", which is mandatory but not binding and is even subject to positive administrative silence if it is not resolved within the legal term (art. 96 LOAF, art. 18 RLOAF No. 2);

(v) *Parliamentary intervention*: Once the BCV's opinion has been issued-or tacitly approved in its absence-the Minister of Finance will submit said opinion, along with an optional technical analysis of the National Public Credit Office to the *Permanent Finance Commission* of the National Assembly, which will consider the operation and approve it through a non-legislative act -subject to a special internal procedure-which, if not produced, will imply a tacit approval of the operation (Art. 18, RLOAF No. 2).

(vi) *National Office of Public Credit:* representing the National Executive, it will carry out public debt operations (issuance of national public debt securities or execution of any other financing contracts).

1.5. Current Status of Venezuela's External Public Debt

1.5.1. Amount

The current amount of external public debt is due to the increase in public spending between 2003 and 2007, during the *Chávez* administration which opted for loans to finance a variety of social projects[58] that raised the debt to US$113 billion by 2013.[59] That sum increased due to the 2024 default resulting from the unilateral suspension of coupon and principal payments on the bonds, as well as the failure to pay court-ordered judgments, arbitration awards, PDVSA liabilities, and other

[58] Pargas Mujica, Luis, "Analysis of Venezuela public debt during the period 1999-2019", *Revista Alternativas de la Universidad Católica de Santiago de Guayaquil,* Vol. 20-1, Guayaquil, 2019.

[59] Vera, Leonardo, "The external public debt that ruined a country, jumps once again into the arena", *PolitikaUcab - Journal of the Center for Political Studies,* Andrés Bello Catholic University, Caracas, 2020.

international obligations that inflated its amount. Presently, Venezuela's external public debt is estimated to be at around US$175 billion.[60]

1.5.2. Sources

Venezuela's current external public debt has at least the following sources:[61]

(i) Financial Debt	• Sovereign bonds (Republic) • PDVSA Bonds (unsecured, guaranteed by Citgo shares, etc.) • Elecar, Sidetur, Corpoelec Bonds
(ii) Multilateral organizations	• Inter-American Development Bank (IDB) • Andean Development Corporation (CAF)
(iii) Bilateral International Agreements	• Agreements of the "Chinese Fund" • Financing - China Development Bank[62] • Oil-for-loan contracts - Russian company Rosneft • Financing - Japan Bank for International Cooperation
(iv) Court rulings	• Judgments in the enforcement phase • Arbitral awards in execution • Pending arbitrations (ICSID and others)
(v) Contractual & Claims	• Wide range of claims against the Republic • Commercial debt (State liabilities) • PDVSA's liabilities

60 Although difficult to determine, by the beginning of 2026 the sum is estimated to be between US$150 billion and US$175 billion, a consensual amount, with its maximum limit estimated at US$200 billion.

61 Santos, Miguel, "Venezuela: Anatomy of a Collapse and a Roadmap for Reconstruction", presentation at the forum "The Venezuela That Is Coming. Political and Economic Solutions", at Andrés Bello University, Chile, 2019. In June 2024, Italiani and Pettersson published the document "Refinancing Venezuela's Debt: Local Legal and Policy Issues" in *The Guide to Restructuring – 3rd Ed.*, LatinLawyer Insight, June, 2024, which contains more recent data.

62 Weisbrot and Johnston highlight: "*Since 2007, Venezuela has also borrowed from China under a set of arrangements that is somewhat complicated. Total borrowing has been $36 billion; according to the Ministry of Petroleum and Mining, $13.5 billion has been repaid. Of the remaining $22.5 billion, $20 billion has been borrowed under the Gran Volume program. These loans pay interest rates of LIBOR plus 1-2 percent, which is far below the*

Although research organizations have attempted to document its exact amount,[63] it is prudent to maintain that all analyses of Venezuela's external public debt face a common problem: the lack of a clear definition of the range of liabilities assumed by the country as external public debt.[64] This means that our study relies on approximations that, even when conservative, yield quite high figures.

1.5.3. Debt-to-GDP ratio

Generally, the ability to service debt and partially repay its principal is based, among other factors, on the *debt-to-GDP ratio,* which, in the case of Venezuela, reached a *ratio* exceeding 200%.[65] These contrasts sharply with other countries that have defaulted recently or maintain significant debts.

- *Greece,* which defaulted in 2011, reflected a debt-to-GDP ratio of 175%.[66]
- *Argentina:* which, for the default of 2019, yielded a debt/GDP ratio of 102%.[67]
- Colombia, which has not been in default, showed a debt/GDP ratio of 44% for 2024, with an external public debt almost equal to that of Venezuela.[68]

---

rate on most others. Venezuelan government borrowing. These interest payments would take up about 0.5 to 0.7 percent of public sector export earnings for 2012. Even with another $2 billion per year for amortization, this wouldn't add too much to Venezuela's debt service burden. Cf.: Weisbrot, Mark and Johnston, Jake, *Venezuela's Economic Recovery: Is it Sustainable?,* Center for Economic and Policy Research, London, 2012.

63 As reported by the Public Spending Observatory of the Center for the Dissemination of Economic Knowledge for Freedom (CEDICE), reports on external debt are available at: https://cedice.org.ve/ogp/deuda-externa/

64 As an example, experts point out that it is possible that in the list contained herein, there may even be duplication of the concept, in the sense that the same sum may be part of two claims in different forums.

65 It is worth noting that this same *ratio* was 49% in 2016 and rose to 186% in 2018. *See: Banking and Business* (06/05/2019): https://www.bancaynegocios.com/torino-deuda-externa-venezolana-representa-186-del-pib/

66 Expansion - Datosmacro.com: Public Debt of Greece 2011 (datosmacro.expansion.com/*deuda/Grecia).*

67 Expansion - Datosmacro.com: Argentine Public Debt 2022 (datosmacro.expansion.com/*deuda/Argentina).*

68 Calculated using information from the Bank of the Republic of Colombia (External *Debt Bulletin for the 1st Half of 2024).*

- *Mexico:* with an external debt of US$ 470 billion, it maintained a debt/GDP ratio of 37% until 2025.[69]

Although industrialized countries have shown high percentage ratios,[70] it is worth emphasizing that the determining factor for facing debt repayment is the *projected* GDP within a medium-term economic plan, a complex aspect to determine in the case of Venezuela in the medium term.

1.5.4. Economic Sanctions

Since 2015, the United States government, through the Office of Foreign Assets Control (OFAC) of the Treasury Department,[71] has imposed a series of economic sanctions on the Venezuelan government (officials), as well as on PDVSA and its subsidiaries, to restrict transactions and commercial operations with third parties. These limitations, which were expanded between 2017 and 2020[72] and supported by part of the international community,[73] prevented the Venezuelan government from accessing international capital markets, which in turn made it impossible to renegotiate overdue obligations on PDVSA's sovereign bonds and other debt instruments issued under New York State law.

---

69 Ministry of Finance and Public Credit of Mexico (Bulletin *No. 53, Public debt as of July 2024).*

70 The United Kingdom has a 95.6% external debt ratio excluding public banks (UK *Office for National Statistics, Data for November 2025).*

71 OFAC "administers *and enforces economic and trade sanctions based on US foreign policy and national security goals against targeted foreign countries and regimes, terrorists, international narcotics traffickers, those engaged in activities related to the proliferation of weapons of mass destruction, and other threats to the national security, foreign policy or economy of the United States". Vid.*: https://ofac.treasury.gov/

72 Seelke, Clare, "Venezuela: Overview of US Sanctions Policy", *US Congressional Research Service*, 2020.

73 "*One last important point: at times it will prove very difficult to distinguish from the effect of sanctions and the more general increase in the reputational costs of doing business with the Venezuelan government, a process that I refer to as economic toxification. This is not surprising, because sanctions are in themselves part of that broader toxification process. That is, sanctions would likely never have been imposed had there not emerged a strong belief among influential groups in public opinion that the access of the Venezuelan government to resources should be limited.*" *Cf.:* Rodríguez, Francisco, *Sanctions, Economic Statecraft, and Venezuela's Crisis - Case Study,* Fourth Freedom Forum, 2022, p. 8.

Until the end of 2025, the only legally viable way to carry out any transaction or negotiation has been to obtain a specific and temporary license from the OFAC, a procedure that has slowed down both negotiations and the execution of pending judicial decisions, a fortuitous situation that, nevertheless, has allowed Venezuela to momentarily retain part of its assets.

Even though the OFAC sanctions remain in effect as of the publication date of this study, for methodological purposes we will base the possibility of carrying out a restructuring of Venezuela's external public debt on two premises: first, that this process would necessarily have to be carried out with prior international consensus (insofar as any initiative of this nature would presuppose a special negotiation); and second, that if such consensus were achieved, the economic sanctions would be lifted progressively or, for the purposes of a restructuring, a general license would be obtained, so they would not constitute a potential impediment as long as there is an agreement with OFAC itself and the creditors.

1.5.5. Default and Legal Actions

The data shows that between 2005 and 2017, Venezuela continued to partially service its debt, that is, to pay principal and interest on both its bonds and other obligations. However, between 2017 and 2018, the country entered into *selective default* by suspending payments on most of its international obligations, but continuing to pay bonds, especially the PDVSA 2020 Bonds and other loans.[74] Then, in October 2019, Venezuela entered into full default, generalized with respect to almost all of its obligations[75] and, in particular, with those related to interest payments on all bond issues, sovereign and PDVSA 2020 (the latter guaranteed with 50.1% of *Citgo Holding 's shares* as collateral).

---

74 This "*continuity* [in debt service payments] *changed during 2018, culminating in a kind of selective default for the first time in its history, within international financial markets. Or, to put it another way, Venezuela has opted to pay its debt very selectively, through the payment of bond issues guaranteed by the shares of its company CITGO Holding Inc., in order not to lose this important asset due to non-payment of its debts"*. Pargas Mujica, Luis, *Op. Cit.*, p. 58.

75 *Standard & Poor's* rating of Venezuela's long-term and short-term sovereign debt in foreign currency.

This suspension of payments resulted in multiple legal actions to claim payment with the intention of taking control of these shares, in different jurisdictions abroad and, particularly in the *District Court for the Southern District of New York* of the State of New York, by virtue of the fact that all recent bond issuances (17 series of Sovereign Bonds with maturities from 2018 to 2038 and at least 13 series of PDVSA Bonds with maturities from 2017 to 2037), are governed by their *prospectuses* (*listing memorandums* or *offering circulars* according to the series)[76] by the legislation of the State of New York.[77]

Given the potential expiration of legal actions related to the bonds, which are governed by both Venezuelan law, which stipulates a 10-year statute of limitations for principal and 3 years for interest, according to the Organic Law of Financial Administration (LOAF), and New York State law, which establishes a 6-year statute of limitations for breaches of contract, including the non-payment of a *default bond,*[78] the Republic agreed on March 30, 2023, to *suspend the statute of limitations for sovereign und PDVSA bonds* as a control measure to prevent the proliferation of lawsuits for non-payment[79]. A potential seizure of

---

76 The term *prospectus* is commonly used in United States legislation to refer to the document of conditions in public markets, and the term *memorandum* - also called *offering circular* - is used for offers that must be approved or registered with the *US Securities and Exchange Commission* (SEC).

77 *Offering circular* issuance of Sovereign Bonds 2018 and later.

78 In New York State Law, Bonds are governed by the *Civil Practice Law & Rules* (NY *CPLR)*, including the statute of limitations for demanding payment of overdue or *defaulted bonds*. This is in accordance with the corollary "*to the extent permitted by applicable law*" in their *offering circulars* and/or *listing memoranda* regarding such time limits. Section 213, Article 2 (Limitations *of Time)*, of the *Civil Practice Law & Rules* (NY *CPLR)* The statute of limitations in the State of New York is six (6) years for breach of contract-which would include *default on a bond.* NY CPLR § 213 [2]: "*Actions to be commenced within six years: where not otherwise provided for; on contract; on sealed instrument; on bond or note, and mortgage upon real property; by state based on misappropriation of public property; based on mistake; by corporation against director, officer or stockholder; based on fraud*".

79 Subsequently, on August 8, 2023, the so-called 2016 National Assembly also announced the suspension of the statute of limitations for the Bonds, under terms identical to those proposed by the Republic and PDVSA. However, on October 11, 2023, some Bondholders, together with the PDVSA Ad Hoc Board of Directors appointed by the 2016 National Assembly, filed a request for a ruling from the Supreme Tribunal of the State of New York regarding the validity of the suspension of the Bonds' statute of limitations, as announced by the 2016 National Assembly. This request focused primarily on the effectiveness of an

Citgo 's shares and assets due to non-payment on bonds secured by its shares, resulting from a situation that has gone from delicate to volatile (since another percentage of its shares is part of a guarantee in favor of *Rosneft*),[80] would be a blow to the national economy.

In any case, in addition to the already high number of lawsuits filed abroad since the end of 2019 due to the *default,* which continue to this day, circumventing the application of American and Venezuelan legislation,[81] there are also legal actions for non-compliance with other non-financial extra-contractual external debt liabilities (e.g.: *awards and judgments*) that have already been declared in favor of the creditors, which has culminated in the virtual loss of Citgo, in view of the auction of shares of the foreign company *PDV Holdings,* a subsidiary of PDVSA and owner of Citgo, ordered by a judge of the State of Delaware as a consequence of the judicial execution of a substantial 2016 award.[82]

Now, regarding this point of legal actions concerning PDVSA 2020 Bonds and others, we have sought to be more specific, since: (i) on one hand, there are important works by various authors that discuss this in detail;[83] and (ii) on the other hand, we emphasize that in this work

---

agreement between the parties (Bondholders and PDVSA, through its Ad Hoc Board of Directors recognized in the United States) concerning the suspension of the Bonds' statute of limitations (a *tolling agreement).*

80 In addition to the bonds guaranteed by 50.1% of its shares, we reiterate that the remaining 49.9% of its shares constitute a guarantee of a loan made to PDVSA by the Russian state oil company *Rosneft.*

81 Decision of the *US Court of Appeals for the Second Circuit* of July 3, 2024 in Case 20-3858, *PDVSA, et al. v. MUFG Union Bank, GLAS Americas,* whereby it vacated with remand the *summary judgment* of the *District Court for Southern District of New York* (Judge Polk Failla) and ordered said court to consider the application of Venezuelan law regarding the validity of the issuance of the PDVSA 2020 Bonds, a matter that is pending in the *District Court for Southern District of New York. York.* This decision, expected by analysts and the creditors themselves, will involve studying Venezuelan legislation pertaining to the legality of the bond issuance, an aspect, as we have said, that has been much debated.

82 This concerns the execution of the arbitration award obtained by the Canadian mining company *Crystallex International Corporation* against the Republic in April 2016 (ICSID *No. ARB(AF)/11/2*), which ordered Venezuela to pay US$1.2 billion plus interest for the expropriation without compensation of a gold mine. According to recent information (January 8, 2026), Venezuela initiated legal action in December before the Third Circuit Court to overturn an order authorizing the sale of nearly US$6 billion worth of Citgo.

83 In this regard, *see:* Rengel Núñez, Pedro, "The notorious case of the PDVSA 2020 bonds", in *Revista Venezolana de Derecho Mercantil,* No. 5, 2020, pp. 35-58; and Hernández, José

we want to refer to *macro* or general aspects related to the possibility of restructuring the debt in a comprehensive manner, excluding in this case a specific examination of the legitimacy of certain claims in litigation and all the legal theories that accompany them, all under the idea that if the nation could indeed initiate this important process, the Republic *must* incorporate into the process all those judicial and arbitral rulings, in addition to the overdue financial debts arising from the bonds and the bilateral commitments acquired, carrying out a process that is, to the extent possible, *universal*.

Indeed, one advantage we see in a comprehensive restructuring process for all parties involved would be the judicial clearance of the multitude of pending actions against Venezuela, since such a process would constitute an attractive pole whose convenience, both for the creditors and for the country, would be predictable if the restructuring is carried out in a suitable and systematic manner according to the guidelines we propose in this study.

II. THE RESTRUCTURING OF EXTERNAL PUBLIC DEBT

2.1. Background

Default has been linked to the very origin of external debt since the beginning of trade, but it was with the mercantile boom of the imperial powers, that significant defaults on sovereign debt by the kingdoms of France, Spain, and Portugal in the mid-16th century, and by Prussia in the 17th century,[84] generated major debt restructuring processes, initially defined as changes in the terms of debt service payments (strictly speaking, today they would be considered *refinancings.*)[85] As we have seen, restructurings in our case began while still within the *Gran Colombia* (1822 and 1824). As a sovereign nation, Venezuela was forced

Ignacio, "Regarding the case of the PDVSA 2020 bonds and the interapplication of commercial and constitutional law", in *Revista Venezolana de Derecho Mercantil,* No. 6, 2021, pp. 105-133.

84 *See:* Reinhart, Carmen; Rogoff, Kenneth; Savastano, Miguel, "Debt Intolerance" in *Brookings Papers on Economic Activity,* Vol. 1, 1-74, 2003.

85 *See:* Kotze, Antonie, "Debt, Defaults and Crises: A Historical Perspective" (working paper), *Financial Chaos Theory Pty. Ltd.*, 2015.

to undertake at least ten processes of restructuring and/or refinancing its external debt, from *Páez* (1840) to *Castro* (1903). However, we are interested here in detailing two relatively recent processes.

2.1.1. Venezuela's 1985 Debt Restructuring

As we have already explained, during the first year of the Lusinchi administration (1985), Venezuela was forced to undergo a restructuring process due to the reluctance of foreign creditor banks to agree to contractual refinancings negotiated with the country without the presence of the IMF. This led to the initiation of a coordinated process with that multilateral organization, which imposed significant austerity measures on the government.

Although the government did not adopt all the measures suggested by the IMF, it did present a plan to reduce public spending which, combined with the devaluation of the *Bolívar*, was considered sufficient to increase financial confidence among its creditors.[86] This led to an unprecedented debt restructuring agreement in Latin America, which was celebrated by the United States as a macroeconomic stabilization achievement in the region.[87] However, given the need to agree to deferrals of principal payments, its implementation extended until 1987, culminating in the presidential decree that finally implemented the *conversion of the restructured debt.*[88]

86 Looney, Robert, "Venezuela's Economic Crisis: Origins and Successes in Stabilization", *Journal of Social, Political and Economic Studies,* Council for Social and Economic Studies, 1986, pp 327-337.

87 McCoy, Jennifer, "The Politics of Adjustment: Labor and the Venezuelan Debt Crisis", *Journal of Interamerican Studies and World Affairs,* V. 28-4, Cambridge University Press, 1987, p. 103.

88 "*Venezuela concluded the negotiation process with its creditor banks in May 1985. The contracts (thirteen in total), signed at the beginning of the following year, contemplated the restructuring of the Republic's debt (both direct and that assumed by 37 public entities), as well as the debt of the companies and decentralized entities that signed the agreements, with the Republic as the guarantee. The amount of these operations reached USD 20.8 billion, corresponding to maturities between 1983 and 1988, with an amortization period of twelve years and six months, without a grace period. Debt amortization began with an initial down payment of USD 750 million, which was approximately 90% covered in 1986*". *Cf.*: Hernández Delfino, Carlos, "The Baker Plan for Debt: An Outline for an Evaluation," *Prodavinci,* Caracas, 2021.

2.1.2. Venezuela's 1990 Financing Plan

The second restructuring process was more complex and far-reaching. It began after the first process concluded, during the second administration of Carlos Andrés Pérez (1989-1990), as part of the *Brady Plan*. Through this process, Venezuela refinanced US$19.7 billions by issuing sovereign bonds with new terms and improved guarantees. This allowed the country to significantly reduce its debt and temporarily alleviate its debt service burden, while also providing the new bonds with greater flexibility for the international market.[89]

2.2. Debt Restructuring in Comparative Law

As WALKER argues, there are few and exceptional countries that lack external public debt, since most nations resort to international financing to cover a significant portion of their public spending,[90] which explains why sovereign debt has been recognized by the United Nations as a problem of *global impact.*[91] The universality of external debt entails a multiplicity of restructuring processes whose impact on the international stage is so frequent today that relevant actors from the World Bank and the IMF -such as KRUEGER- have insisted for years on the need to design an international legal system that provides an adequate framework especially for these processes, not only for the benefit of creditors, but also to safeguard and protect vulnerable economies.[92]

In the absence of an internationally regulated and agreed-upon process, each restructuring is subject to national legal mechanisms (*domestic legislation)* because it naturally involves acts or processes regulated by domestic public law and, more specifically, by local administrative

89 On the topic in general, *see:* Hernández Delfino, Carlos, "Venezuela and the Brady Initiative", *Prodavinci,* Caracas, 2021.

90 Walker, Mark, "Thoughts *on the Possible Restructuring of Venezuelan Debt"* (interview*)*, LEC Abogados, Caracas, 2023.

91 According to data from the *United Nations Conference on Trade and Development (UNCTAD),* global public debt reached a record high of $97 trillion in 2023. Although public debt in developing countries represented less than a third of the total, since 2010 it has grown twice as fast as in developed economies. See: https://unctad.org/publication/world-of-debt

92 Krueger, Anne, *A New Approach To Sovereign Debt Restructuring,* International Monetary Fund, Washington, 2002.

law; but additionally, it usually requires the application of foreign law - often American - since a large part of the contracts and, especially, the securities (*bonds*), are issued in the international market.

In any case, sovereign debt restructurings have been common practice in developing economies, notably in Latin America --especially Argentina- certain European countries -Greece and Russia- and more vulnerable economies in the Middle East and Africa. We will analyze the following cases in chronological order:

2.2.1. Argentina (2001)

One process that deserves attention was that carried out by *Argentina* (2001-2002), a country that, after having faced multiple economic crises since 1989, incurred a historic massive *default* on its sovereign debt in 2001, which triggered a political and economic crisis (popular protests, resignation of President *De la Rúa)* that lasted for several years with significant consequences.

Argentina's external debt, composed of a variety of bonds denominated in different currencies, became unsustainable, so the government initiated a refinancing called the "*mega-swap*". However, this did not contain the crisis and led to a default that necessitated a restructuring carried out between 2001 and 2005, with the participation of local bondholders and, in a later phase, international creditors. The process involved a nominal *haircut* of up to 66% of the debt, and by 2005, the government had already been able to restructure around 75% of its debt (offering new bonds at a loss). The process, which included the participation, at least initially, of the IMF-an organization that, despite having ceased its financing programs after the crisis, continued to advise on the restructuring-could not alleviate the entire burden of external debt, as evidenced by the new default and restructuring between 2018 and 2020.

2.2.2. Uruguay (2003)

We briefly mention, as an example of a successful and relatively sustainable restructuring, the case of *Uruguay,* which, as a result of the region's crisis in 2001-2002, opted for a preventive restructuring in the face of the possibility of *default.* This involved a "voluntary exchange" to extend maturity dates without reducing the nominal value of the bonds, which allowed for an orderly process with the voluntary participation of at least 90% of the creditors, avoiding significant international litigation.

2.2.3. Iraq (2003)

Iraqi debt restructuring, carried out between 2003 and 2006, deserves attention due to its relative similarity to the Venezuelan case and a particular circumstance in its execution regarding debt *haircuts.* Firstly, because at the time it was considered one of the most complex and extensive restructurings in modern history, prompting the United Nations Security Council and the United States government to enact measures to protect Iraq's assets from international creditors. These aspects bear some resemblance to the Venezuelan case, which, in addition to being unprecedented, has been the initial reason for measures to safeguard assets against creditors before the start of a restructuring, as evidenced by the presidential executive order of January 9, 2026.[93] Secondly, we highlight this example because in the case of Iraq, nominal *haircuts* of up to 80% were proposed for certain liabilities (subject to prior agreement with the *Paris Club*), being the highest debt reduction example in recent restructurings (only comparable to the 66% haircuts carried out in the Argentine restructuring).[94]

2.2.4. Greece (2009)

Because of its magnitude and the impact it had on the European Union and the financial world, it is worth mentioning the case of *Greece* (2009-2012), whose restructuring process was considered the most important in recent times, due to its complexity, extent and the participation of the European Commission, the IMF and other multilateral organizations, as well as the opinions of the most eminent economists worldwide -such as KRUGMAN or STIGLITZ- who discussed the topic extensively in various articles and forums and questioned not only local

93 Safeguarding Venezuelan Oil Revenue for the Good of the American and Venezuelan People. *Vid.*: https://www.whitehouse.gov/presidential-actions/2026/01/safeguarding-venezuelan-oil-revenue-for-the-good-of-the-american-and-venezuelan-people/

94 Hinrichsen, Simon, "The Iraq sovereign debt restructuring", in *Capital Markets Law Journal,* Vol. 16 (1), January 2021.

or European institutional failures that motivated the financial crisis, but even the very adoption of the euro by economies such as Greece.[95]

As a very brief historical summary, the Greek external debt crisis had its economic origins in 2000, but it erupted in 2009 as a result of the government's recognition that its fiscal deficit was much larger than originally reported to international organizations, creditors, and the international community in general.[96] This triggered alarm in international financial markets and forced the European Union, together with the IMF, to carry out a *financial rescue operation,* which entailed the imposition of severe austerity measures.[97]

What is relevant for the purposes of our study is that from 2010 onwards-and for several years afterward-Greece was subject to successive financial bailouts (both public and private) and was forced to undertake various refinancing processes. The restructuring process carried out in 2012 was particularly significant, involving a *reduction* of approximately €100 billion in private debt. This allowed Greece to lessen its burden and stabilize its economy, but it also had significant economic and political consequences.[98] Although these successive processes were considered failures in several instances, the Greek economy eventually regained stability, though it remains highly vulnerable due to a combination of structural factors and inefficient political management. From the Greek experience, however, we can draw two important lessons:

---

95 Karanasos, Menelaos, Koutroumpis, Panagiotis, Hatgioannides, John, *et al.*, "The Greek Dra(ch)ma: 5 Years of Austerity. The Three Economists' View and a Comment", *Papers on Greece and Southeast Europe,* No. 113, Hellenic Observatory of the London School of Economics, London, 2017.

96 The cited authors highlight that: "*During the period 2000-2008 there was an influx of cheap loans and large amounts of capital that created the boom. The Greek government for many years borrowed and spent beyond the country's capabilities*". They then maintain that "*...as a result of the financial crisis, debt to GDP ratios started to increase (Greece's debt was 117% of its GDP). When the boom turned into a bust, there was a massive outflow of liquidity when investors massively sold Greek government bonds pushing interest rates to unsustainably high levels. Due to a poorly designed euro, money during the crisis flew from the weak country's (that is Greece) banks to the strong, leading to divergence...*", *Idem.*, p. 5.

97 Buchheit, Lee, and Gulati, Mitu, "How to Restructure Greek Debt", *Op. cit.*

98 Katsikas, Dimitris, "The Greek economic crisis of 2012" in *CIDOB International Yearbook 2013,* p. 197 et seq.

(i) That the restructuring required debt forgiveness for bondholders, a flexible offer from the government (exchanges with credit improvements and promissory notes issued by the European Financial Stability Facility) and the activation of *collective action clauses* (CACs) that forced creditors to be part of the process to give it effectiveness; and

(ii) In that case, there was significant participation from the IMF, assisted by the *European Commission* and the *European Central Bank,*[99] which contributed to the financial rescue and the creation of the *Financial Stability Fund* that allowed the gradual recovery of the Greek economy from 2012 onwards, subject to the implementation of changes in its fiscal policy.[100]

2.2.5. Other cases

Additionally, we note that debt restructurings in *Jamaica, Russia, Ecuador, Pakistan,* and *Ivory Coast* highlight the importance of cooperation with multilateral organizations and the implementation of structural reforms to achieve sustainable economic stability. Jamaica and Pakistan demonstrated that a collaborative approach and international oversight can facilitate restructurings without significant haircuts, while Ecuador showed that unilateral renegotiation can be effective in the short term but potentially reputationally damaging in the long run. On the other hand, robust economic recovery, such as Russia's oil-driven recovery, was also key to restoring market confidence.

2.3. Theoretical Framework of Debt Restructuring

2.3.1. Conceptualization of Restructuring and Refinancing

Both terms refer to the reorganization of liabilities, but although there is no universally accepted definition, we emphasize that they often have different meanings, especially regarding their scope and use in

[99] A group of institutions that jointly participated in the financial bailouts of the European crises and which Mario Monti, former Prime Minister of Italy, and others, pejoratively referred to as the *Troika.*

[100] Carrasquero, Andrés; Escovar, Ramón; Campos, Mariana; and Freitas, Víctor, *Op. cit.*

public and international law. We will attempt here to provide a consensus definition:

a) **Refinancing:** In the private and commercial sphere, the term *refinancing* is often used to refer to the modification of financial conditions through agreements that generate new debt.[101]

b) **Restructuring:** It typically refers to a *process- rather than a mere transaction-* involving the renegotiation of existing debt terms to restore repayment capacity and ensure the economic sustainability of both the debtor and the repayment system.[102] It encompasses complex mechanisms that go beyond simply modifying financial conditions (such as refinancing) and usually includes a wide range of operations that frequently involve one or more refinancings,[103] in addition to other simultaneous mechanisms.[104] Sovereign restructurings typically include *refinancings* through debt rescheduling with extended maturities and new, reduced interest rates; but also, reductions in the face value of existing instruments; as well as debt buybacks (exchanging outstanding debt instruments for discounted cash), all through legal processes and one or more new sovereign debt contracts.[105] In addition to its breadth, the doctrine recog-

[101] "Refinancing *existing debt seems to be one of the most important, if not the first, reason to issue new debt". Cf.:* Forte, Santiago, and Peña, Juan, "Debt refinancing and credit risk" in *Spanish Review of Financial Economics,* Vol. 9-1, 2011.

[102] Sachs, Jeffrey, *The End of Poverty: Economic Possibilities for Our Time,* Penguin, New York, 2005.

[103] "*Macro policies are an essential feature as they bound the feasible timing of debt restructuring and guide key judgments on individual firm viability. For example, reduction in interest rates can spur refinancing, which can provide debt servicing relief" ... Cf.:* Laryea, Thomas, *Approaches to Corporate Debt Restructuring in the Wake of Financial Crises,* IMF Staff Position Note, International Monetary Fund, Washington, 2010.

[104] Humes points out in this regard that: "*In addition to modifying contractual payment terms, there is, depending on the profile of the debtor country, often substantial scope for the utilization of additional tools such as debt/equity swaps, as well as other equity-like or contingent payment instruments including GDP-or commodity-linked warrants and Value Recovery Instruments*". *Vine.:* Humes, Hans, "*Thoughts on the Possible Restructuring of Venezuelan Debt*", interview published in LEC Abogados, Caracas, 2023, available at: https://www.lec.com.ve/en/home/#blog

[105] "*While there is no universally accepted definition, a sovereign debt restructuring can be defined as an exchange of outstanding sovereign debt instruments, such as loans or bonds, for new debt instruments or cash through a legal process. Sovereign debt, here, refers to*

nizes that, in the context of sovereign debt, restructuring pursues broader objectives, not only aimed at alleviating debt service, but also at ensuring operational continuity[106] and some degree of long-term *economic sustainability.*[107]

Apart from terminological clarifications -since, as we saw, every restructuring will involve refinancing- both mechanisms, which may vary in their complexity, have been an integral part of sovereign public debt since its inception, as evidenced in the historical cases we have discussed.

2.3.2. Treatment in Venezuela

In the specific case of Venezuela, both terms have been used almost interchangeably (perhaps because the processes have been more similar to *refinancings* of existing debt that have resulted from previous consolidations); however, strictly speaking, *restructuring refers to broader and more complex processes that include various financial modification operations,* which suggests that its approach will be more comprehensive and will address multiple dimensions linked to the sustainability of the sovereign debt problem,[108] which is why the common terminology in the international arena refers, instead of refinancing, to ***sovereign debt restructuring.***[109]

---

debt issued or guaranteed by the government of a sovereign state. [...] One can generally distinguish two main elements in a debt restructuring: Debt rescheduling, which can be defined as a lengthening of maturities of the old debt, possibly involving lower interest rates. Debt rescheduling imply debt relief, as they shift contractual payments into the future; and Debt reduction, which can be defined as a reduction in the face (nominal) value of the old instruments (e.g, from US$ 100 to US$ 80). Cf.: Das, Udaibir, Papaioannou, Michael G., and Trebesch, Christoph, *Sovereign Debt Restructurings 1950–2010: Concepts, Literature Survey, and Stylized Facts,* IMF Working, International Monetary Fund.

106 International Monetary Fund, *World Economic Outlook,* 2020.

107 Ocampo, José Antonio, "The Urgency of Sovereign-Debt Restructuring" in *Project Syndicate,* April, 2024.

108 According to Stiglitz, "the *restructuring of sovereign debt is carried out with the ultimate goal of restoring public debt sustainability with a high probability". Cf.*: Guzmán, Martín and Stiglitz, Joseph, *A "Soft Law" Mechanism for Sovereign Debt Restructuring: Based on UN Principles,* Friedrich Ebert Stiftung, New York, 2016.

109 This is how it is used in all documents of international organizations and multilateral bodies, as can be seen in the United Nations (UN) chapter on *Sovereign Debt Restructuring.*

We note that in the restructuring processes carried out by the Republic in 1985 and 1990, both terms were used without much distinction: thus, on the one hand, the special law that authorized the first process referred expressly to the *General Program for Refinancing* of debt that was due in 1983-84,[110] but the agreements made with the creditors were called *Restructuring Agreements*[111] on the other hand, we observe that the special law that initiated the process in 1990 again referred to operations intended to *refinance external public debt,*[112] but Decree No. 1,261 containing the so-called "*Financial Plan*", alluded to the "*restructured or restructuring-able*" external debt obligations that were assumed by the Republic with the conversion of debt into bonds. Seen in retrospect, they were genuine[113] *sovereign restructuring* processes that certainly involved refinancing, but also made use of other broader financial mechanisms, which is why the normative terminology was used in an analogous and perhaps ambiguous way.

2.3.3. Restructuring in the Public Sector Financial Management System

Although it might appear that the conceptualization of both notions was intended to be clarified through the *Organic Law of Public Sector Financial Administration* ("LOAF") of 2000, successively amended until 2016, the truth is that the legislator did not make any significant technical distinction, merely indicating that both processes, which constitute public credit operations, would encompass the consolidation, unification, conversion, and "*any other form*" of debt refinancing or restructuring (Art. 80, No. 5). Subsequently, the Administration sought to be more precise in Regulation No. 2 of the LOAF (or "RLOAF No. 2"),[114] which developed the *Public Credit System,* by clarifying these notions.

---

110 Official Gazette No. 3,253 of September 14, 1983, partially amended by Gazette No. 3,471 Extraordinary of August 6, 1984.

111 Such was the case of the agreement signed with *Chase Manhattan* that regulated the payment terms of the "*Re-Loan Facility Agreement*" in that process.

112 Official Gazette No. 34,558 of September 21, 1990.

113 Official Gazette No. 34,598 of November 20, 1990.

114 Official Gazette No. 38,117 of January 28, 2005.

In accordance with this regulatory framework, ***restructuring*** will be a public credit operation of the Republic (and/or the other entities authorized by the LOAF) through which *agreements are entered into* with its financial creditors to extinguish an existing debt (including interest) and simultaneously contract new debt (art. 3, no. 33); and ***refinancing*** will be a *set of* public credit operations of the Republic (and/or the other entities authorized by the LOAF) through which *new* public debt is issued to pay, exchange, cancel, redeem, or repurchase pre-existing public debt (art. 3, no. 34).

According to the regulatory body-that is, the Administration- *new debt will be issued* in both cases: in restructuring through direct novation (or simultaneous contracts for extinguishment and assumption of obligation) and, in the case of refinancing, through modification of the nature of the original debt instrument. However, we note that these regulatory definitions proved imprecise and apparently ended up confusing both terms-at least from the perspective of international legal doctrine, where restructuring is the process and refinancing is a modality-an aspect that, while noteworthy, does not affect the effectiveness of these mechanisms.

Indeed, it could even be argued that this terminological rigor, in the case of Venezuela, loses some importance since the regulation itself determined that both restructuring and refinancing are carried out through a wide range of operations, which are properly the practical mechanisms for modifying the debt:

(i) Consolidation (art. 3, no. 8);
(ii) Unification (Art. 3, No. 39);
(iii) Conversion (art. 3, no. 11);
(iv) Call (art. 3, no. 37);
(v) Exchange (art. 3, no. 4); and
(vi) Buyback (art. 3, no. 32).

2.4. Legal Nature of Debt Restructuring

2.4.1. Public Credit Operation

Although *strictly speaking* not all the aforementioned operations contemplated by the legislator in the LOAF (Organic Law of Public Finance) imply the assumption of new debts from a technical standpoint (since not all constitute new eventual cash outlays),[115] they are all part of restructuring and/or refinancing processes, and as such are considered public credit operations. Indeed, the LOAF expressly stipulated *refinancing or restructuring* operations (consolidation, conversion, unification, or any other form) as *public credit operations* (Art. 77), and therefore they are subject to the legal provisions of the LOAF and those contained in its Regulation No. 2, as well as other applicable special regulations.

2.4.2. Contract of National Public Interest

Additionally, in the event that the *refinancing or restructuring operations* concern *external debt* of the public sector (i.e.: debt with foreign entities), by binding jurisprudential interpretation of the Constitutional Chamber of the Supreme Tribunal of Justice, that operation will be considered as a *contract of national public interest*[116] and this will result in the jurisprudential imposition of some additional requirements to those provided for in the LOAF.

While it is true that operations other than restructuring may also be of national public interest due to their magnitude and importance-an aspect that will require examining compliance with the jurisprudential conditions for such classification-for the purposes of this study, we will limit ourselves to referring, at this point, to processes of *restructuring external public debt,* as this is the objective of our analysis. Thus, for this specific process, unlike in the other cases covered by the LOAF, a provision in a special debt law will not be required. However, this exception will only apply, as we noted earlier, when the process or operation *seeks to improve the conditions of prior indebtedness* (e.g.: reducing the agreed interest rate, extending the payment term, converting

[115] However, the truth is that in all of them, directly or through a designated financial agent, a new obligation will be subscribed or acquired that will involve the pre-existing ones and that may novate the financial conditions or extinguish them, but will necessarily imply new obligations (and new public credit operations) under new conditions that are understood by the legislator as new sources of future public debt, and hence they are subject to that legislative approval.

[116] Binding jurisprudence of the Constitutional Chamber of the Supreme Tribunal of Justice in the case *Andrés Velásquez, Elías Mata and others.*

external debt into internal debt, reducing cash flow, or allowing savings in financing costs) (Art. 100).

It would seem that this condition is met in most cases, since it is inherent in the initial nature of any restructuring to improve the debtor's conditions, although we leave open the possibility contemplated by the legislator, of the modification of conditions that could be for us an "improvement", but that are not included in that list of the LOAF (or of operations that do not have those specific objectives), in which case the restructuring must be foreseen in the debt law, presumably because new debts will be incurred *per se*.

2.5. Internal Procedure applicable to Debt Restructuring

Having overcome this issue that originates in any restructuring process, the main additional requirement imposed by virtue of the national public interest nature of external debt will be the *authorization* by way of *a Parliamentary Agreement* of the National Assembly when so provided by law: this was determined by the Constitutional Chamber of the Supreme Tribunal of Justice in a judgment of June 13, 2001 (Case: *William Lara*), in interpretation of articles 150, 154 and 198.9 of the Constitution, referring to contracts of national public interest due to cooperation agreements with Cuba, in which the restrictive nature of the interpretation of parliamentary control over the contracting activity of the Public Administration was affirmed.[117]

Thus, this parliamentary intervention, when determined by law, would take place after the operation has been considered by the *Standing Committee on Finance,* a condition that, in our opinion, should be applied even to previously approved processes, as they are also of national public interest.[118] Restructurings authorized by the National

117 In general, the legislative oversight exercised by the National Assembly must be interpreted *restrictively* and cannot interfere with the development of administrative activity or constitute an impediment to its work, by virtue of the *principle of separation of powers* (Art. 136, Const.), which establishes that each branch of government has its own functions but has the duty to collaborate with one another to achieve the aims of the State. Additionally, in this specific case, said oversight will be interpreted restrictively because it constitutes a *limitation on the Administration's freedom to enter into contracts.*

118 In the case of public credit operations contracts already authorized by *the Special Law on Annual Indebtedness* that have not been fully disbursed, it is understood that these

Assembly must be submitted to the Attorney General's Office for its non-binding opinion on the appropriateness of the operation, given the national interests involved in the process and under the principle that this body safeguards the nation's judicial interests (Art. 11, Organic Law of the Attorney General's Office).

In summary, we can recap that any restructuring of external public debt must *necessarily follow* these steps:

(i) Provision in the debt law if it does not seek to improve existing conditions or has another purpose;

(ii) Request from the National Office of Public Credit and the Vice Minister of Financial Management to the Minister of Finance to initiate the procedure;

(iii) Presidential Approval in the Council of Ministers;

(iv) Request - but not approval - for a technical opinion from the BCV;

(v) Consideration-but not approval-by the Standing Committee on Finance of the National Assembly; and

(vi) Authorization of the National Assembly by means *of a parliamentary agreement* when determined by law.

Compliance with this complex procedure is relevant to determining the validity of external public debt operations assumed by the Republic or state-owned companies, whether as autonomous debt operations or as a result of refinancing or restructuring, an aspect that is of vital importance in the case of PDVSA 2020 Bonds.

III. ON THE POSSIBILITY OF RESTRUCTURING VENEZUELA'S EXTERNAL PUBLIC DEBT

The preceding analysis is essential for understanding the complexity of Venezuela's external public debt, the diverse international pro-

do not require additional authorization from the National Assembly for disbursements in subsequent years, since these debt operations were already controlled and contemplated in the respective Law. However, as in the previous case, even though they do not require authorization by law, if these contracts form part of a refinancing or restructuring agreement *for public debt with foreign entities,* they must be authorized by the National Assembly, in accordance with the terms indicated above.

blems that exacerbated it, the possibility that the debt includes unexpected liabilities and commitments that could increase its amount, and the nature of the creditors[119] and the conditions that would theoretically limit its restructuring. However, to avoid this study becoming outdated, we will proceed from the premise that debt restructuring may be possible, albeit conditionally. This possibility, however, does not necessarily mitigate other challenges related to Venezuela's external debt (amount, scope, diversity of creditors, etc.). Therefore, we will seek to analyze and propose mechanisms for carrying out a large-scale restructuring process with structured and coordinated approaches to address immediate challenges and establish the foundations for the country's long-term economic stability and sustainable growth.

For pragmatic purposes, we will avoid delving into specific legal actions (e.g.: legitimacy of the bonds, statute of limitations, forum suitability, among others), as our intention is to present a comprehensive study that does not get lost in the multiple possibilities of defense, but rather focuses on finding a sustainable solution to this complicated and extraordinary situation.

3.1. Doctrinal Proposals (2017-2024)

Most of the authors consulted agree that a comprehensive process of restructuring Venezuelan debt today could be the most extensive in modern history, comparable to that of *Greece,* although undoubtedly more complex, considering the diversity of creditors involved, as well as the associated collateral aspects (guarantees, lawsuits, arbitrations and sanctions), in addition to its broad scope and the international repercussions it entails.

Given this stark warning, it is pertinent to conduct a detailed analysis-to the extent possible, given the space limitations-of the various positions contained in recent studies on the restructuring of Venezuela's

---

[119] As an example, since mid-2024, new lawsuits have been filed against *PDV Holding Inc.*: in Texas, Siemens Energy filed a lawsuit in April; in August, a Delaware judge ordered the auction of the company's shares; in October, part of the shares were awarded to a fund, and a *delay was ordered* due to the emergence of new creditors. The short-term future can be expected to be equally or even more complex, due to creditor pressure and the inevitability of slowing down actions already underway or in the execution phase.

external public debt, prepared between 2017 and 2025 by a diverse group of actors-academics, researchers, financial advisors, and law firms-whose plurality and diversity of areas of specialization will contribute to providing different points of view that will enrich a discussion that, to date, we believe still requires an extensive but urgent debate in the Venezuelan legal forum.

3.1.1. Buchheit and Gulati: *holdouts, CACs and Chapter 15*

We initially highlight the proposal made in 2017 -prior to the *default,* the deepening of the political crisis and the tightening of economic sanctions- by academics Buchheit and Gulati, who participated in the doctrinal discussion of the Greek external debt crisis and studied the complexity that a large-scale restructuring process would entail with the voluntary participation of creditors in Venezuela,[120] a situation that has changed since the massive start of legal actions resulting from the *default*.

Apart from the advisability of updating that study in relation to the *default* and economic sanctions, we highlight the most relevant aspects of its proposal in relation to a possible total restructuring of the debt from financial operations, and in particular of sovereign bonds and PDVSA Bonds:

(i) To determine the potential risk of the actions of *holdout creditors* within the process and ways to discourage their negative actions, highlighting examples in the Argentine and Greek processes, and the difficulty that such groups bring to restructuring strategies.

(ii) Need to know in detail the distinction between the clauses of the Republic sovereign bonds and the PDVSA bonds, especially with regard to the creditors' consensus and the inclusion of *collective action clauses* (hereinafter "CACs").

(iii) The advisability and possibility-until then little discussed-of either initiating bankruptcy proceedings for PDVSA under

[120] Buchheit, Lee, and Gulati, Mitu, "How to Restructure Venezuelan Debt", in *Duke Law School Public Law & Legal Theory Series,* No. 52, August 2017. Buchheit is a professor and participated in the 2012 Greek restructuring and Mitu conducts studies on sovereign debt restructuring in emerging countries.

American legislation (Chapter *15)*, or of creating a new, separate state-owned company capable of assuming, under certain conditions, the new restructured debts, with the financial-and political-complexities that this would entail, an element that we will return to in the study; and

(iv) Incorporate the necessary participation of the IMF and other multilateral organizations to reach a comprehensive agreement with the qualified majority of creditors, which includes the adoption of a national economic adjustment program aimed at correcting structural aspects and underlying problems of the Venezuelan economy.

Their proposal, which brings concrete legal and financial elements to the table (such as examining the clauses of the various bonds and the possibility of reaching agreements and modifications), while highlighting the complexity of this potential process, *does not rule it out as impossible.* They argue that if many conditions are met-conditions that will undoubtedly be difficult to achieve-Venezuela could begin a long and complicated restructuring process. They acknowledge beforehand how difficult it will be, in Venezuela's case, to involve the IMF in the process, given the almost forced animosity with which the country has maintained relations with that organization. However, they believe this situation could change in light of Venezuela's relationship with the United States and the conditions that the US government imposes for accessing the restructuring process.

3.1.2. Moatti and Muci: *audit, debt committee and oil warrants*

A more strategic approach to organization and time management was published in March 2019 by consultants and researchers MOATTI and MUCI in a study conducted under the auspices of the *Harvard Kennedy School of Government,*[121] with input from economist REINHART

[121] Moatti, Thomas, and Muci, Frank, *An Economic Framework for Venezuela's Debt Restructuring,* Harvard Kennedy School, 2019. Moatti is an advisor at *Lazard Frères & Co.,* and Muci is a researcher at the *London School of Economic and Political Science*

and Venezuelan economist HAUSMANN.[122] In this study, the authors outlined a series of observations and practical recommendations for restructuring, among which we highlight the following:

(i) Need to conduct a thorough audit of the debts that make up the external public debt, ensuring transparency and coordination with respect to the different debtor entities and their creditors.

(ii) Define, in advance, the scope and economic framework of the process, establish a legal framework that guarantees legal certainty, protects the seizure of assets abroad, provides flexibility in negotiations, making use of legal procedures without excluding diplomatic options.

(iii) Appoint a *national debt committee* with the authority to address the process comprehensively, composed of the Ministry of Finance, the Public Credit Office, experts (financial, legal and public relations) and representatives of the BCV, PDVSA, among others, to centralize information and negotiations, as well as to serve as a liaison with the IMF.

(iv) Adopt a unified and prudent approach to the legitimacy of debts, to preserve credibility and access to future financing and to efficiently manage public opinion.

(v)Prioritize reconstruction and economic recovery, as debt service could consume the restructuring itself, so it is crucial that any support prioritizes the restoration of crude oil imports.

(vi) Sequencing the restructuring and prioritizing the classes of creditors, avoiding entering into early negotiations with groups of bondholders, which would increase the risk for its main direct creditors (Russia and China), therefore insisting on a priority and staggered negotiation that allows delaying the commitment with market creditors until agreements are reached with bilateral lenders.

(vii) Incorporate *oil warrants* into the negotiations to mitigate the uncertainty associated with fluctuating oil prices, ensuring a fair distribution of benefits between the government and creditors.

---

122 Director of the *Growth Lab* at Harvard University and dedicated to international political economy at the *Harvard Kennedy School.*

This proposal, which stands out for its organizational approach and pragmatism through prudent suggestions that are undoubtedly essential for the start of the process (*e.g.*, financial audit, prior legal framework, creation of a national committee to centralize negotiations), should be taken into account for the purposes of any process, since in addition to its strategic aspect, it highlights the need to prioritize all classes of creditors in a possible negotiation, a crucial matter given the diversity of outstanding commitments and liabilities.

3.1.3. Walker and Cooper: *Chapter 15* and *legislation to revitalize the public sector*

In July 2019, attorneys and advisors WALKER and COOPER published in an internal *journal* of public debt and restructuring of the firm *Cleary Gottlieb,* a practical study that contains a roadmap of steps to follow to address restructuring in Venezuela.[123]

In their analysis, they generally argue for the need for a special legal framework (specifically, a special law for the "Revitalization *of the Venezuelan Public Sector*") and the adoption of United States *Chapter 15 bankruptcy procedures* to resolve PDVSA's liabilities. They also advocate for the adoption of a combination of financial techniques (exit consents, structuring options, and positive and negative incentives) to resolve the Republic's liabilities, emphasizing in both cases the need for the involvement of the IMF, as well as other international financial institutions and the international community in general. The main points highlighted by these authors are as follows:

(i) Creation of a comprehensive legal framework for revitalizing the economy that in turn allows for the restructuring of public debt.

(ii) The strategic reorganization of legal actions against the Republic and PDVSA.

(iii) The need to ensure the greatest possible participation of creditors and to seek mechanisms to discourage "holdouts."

123 Walker, Mark, and Cooper, Richard, "Venezuela's Restructuring: A Path Forward" in *Emerging Markets Restructuring Journal,* Cleary Gottlieb, Summer 2019. Walker is a partner at the firm and Cooper is a director at *Guggenheim Securities, LLC.*

(iv) The participation of the IMF and the Paris Club in the renegotiation of sovereign debt through traditional mechanisms that seek to provide legal certainty.

(v) The incorporation of traditional and novel mechanisms in parallel in the restructuring of sovereign and PDVSA bonds, and their linkage with possible *oil warrants* and other mechanisms linked to oil prices.

3.1.4. Kargman: *haircuts and debt-equity swaps*

In 2020, the American lawyer and consultant KARGMAN published a study in the *Venezuelan Journal of Legislation and Jurisprudence* on the legal and public policy issues to address a restructuring in Venezuela, in which he mentions an element that we consider essential, which is the need for the participation of top-level Venezuelan professionals - especially lawyers and jurists - who "*not only have a technical mastery in (...) key substantive areas, but more importantly, understand that the lives and well-being of almost thirty million Venezuelans are at stake.*"[124]

In his study, the author also agrees on the need to involve the IMF, the World Bank, the IDB, and CAF, among others, given the international dimension of the debt. From this study, we highlight the following points regarding the effects of a restructuring:

(i) The possibility of applying standardized restructuring tools ("haircuts", short-term rescheduling, *oil warrants)* with less orthodox techniques such as debt *-equity swaps,* already proposed in 1990, but with a novel approach that must be compared in light of Venezuelan legislation; and

(ii) The need to protect PDVSA's assets from legal action (a matter that is currently complicated by the large number of ongoing lawsuits), as well as the possibility of initiating bankruptcy proceedings under Venezuelan or American law.

[124] Kargman, Steven, "Venezuela's Potential Debt Restructuring and Economic Recovery Efforts: Some Key Legal and Policy Challenges" in *Revista Venezolana de Legislación y Jurisprudencia,* No. 13, 2020, pp 163-190.

In 2021 the author updated and expanded the detail of his analysis,[125] which is why we suggest reading it, but in general terms these two aspects, added to the need to revitalize the oil industry and diversify the local economy, are what we bring up from our study.

3.1.5. Carrasquero, Escovar *et al.: CACs, IMF and World Bank*

Venezuelan attorneys Carrasquero, Escovar, Campos, and Freitas, who have published several studies on the topic of external debt under the auspices of CEDICE's Public Spending Observatory, conducted an analysis in 2022 of experiences and effective proposals for Venezuelan debt.[126] This study was later complemented in August 2023 by a comparative law revision of similar processes carried out in Uruguay, Greece, Puerto Rico, and Argentina.[127] From these two papers, we highlight the following suggestions and conclusions:

(i) Debt restructuring will have to resort to "non-traditional" mechanisms, such as debt-for-equity swaps in oil companies (this is based on sanctions, but it remains a current proposal).

(ii) The lack of CACs and aggregation in several bonds will make restructuring more difficult (due to holdout creditors).

(iii) The inclusion of the IMF, the World Bank, or the IDB will be necessary to have technical support in negotiations with creditors and to increase the credibility of the process;

(iv) The private sector must participate in the negotiations, with the aim of including as many creditors and bondholders as possible in the process; and

(v) The need to have an experienced economic advisory team at the start of the process, capable of finding sustainable solutions.

---

125 Kargman, Steven, "Venezuela: Prospects for Restructuring Sovereign Debt and Rebuilding a National Economy against the backdrop of a Failing State", in Journal of the *Association of Insolvency & Restructuring Advisors (AIRA),* 2021.

126 Carrasquero, Andrés; Escovar, Ramón; and Campos, Mariana, *The Restructuring of Venezuelan External Debt: Experiences, Limits and Effective Proposals,* CEDICE Libertad, Caracas, 2022. The authors are Venezuelan lawyers and partners of the firm *ESCG Abogados.*

127 Carrasquero, Andrés; Escovar, Ramón; Campos, Mariana; and Freitas, Víctor, *The Restructuring (...), Op. cit.*

3.1.6. Italiani, Omaña and Pettersson: *Chapter 15, new PDVSA, debt-equity swaps*

In June 2024, another group of Venezuelan attorneys, ITALIANI, OMAÑA, and PETTERSSON, made an important contribution regarding the legal aspects of a possible restructuring of Venezuelan debt,[128] from which we summarize the most relevant recommendations for this potential process:

(i) The creation of a modern insolvency regulatory framework aligned with both international practices and foreign bankruptcy laws, which could be applicable to public entities such as PDVSA (whose status as a functionally decentralized public administration entity calls into question the application of even the Venezuelan Commercial Code, much less foreign laws such as *Chapter 15).*

(ii) The need to address the restructuring in a comprehensive manner, involving all creditors, which is considered legally viable, but subject to a macro political commitment, as well as the cooperation of creditors and other parties, raises a political and international issue.

(iii) The possibility - already studied among that group by PETTERSSON in 2019[129]- to establish a new state-owned company, distinct from PDVSA, that will receive the exploration and exploitation rights (primary activities), as well as the hydrocarbon assets and licenses, and that will assume responsibility for the PDVSA bonds as successor, in accordance with the Commercial Code.

(iv) Explore the possibility of debt *-equity swaps* to reduce debt levels and attract foreign investment.

---

[128] Italiani, Fulvio Omaña, Carlos; and Pettersson, Roland, *Op. cit.* The authors are Venezuelan lawyers, partners of *D'Empaire.*

[129] Pettersson and Levin: "A New PDVSA? The Transfer of Venezuela's Oil Assets to a Successor Entity and Fraudulent Conveyance", in *Capital Markets Law Journal,* Oxford University Press, 2019.

3.2. Our Proposal: Guidelines for a Comprehensive Debt Restructuring

3.2.1. Preface. Feasibility of restructuring

After examining doctrinal positions and relevant literature, as well as analyzing the risks and magnitude of the external debt within the context of Venezuelan public law and applicable aspects of international law, we recognize that numerous factors hinder the initiation of a comprehensive restructuring process. However, it is crucial to point out that none of these factors constitutes an absolute legal or material impossibility that precludes the viability of this process. Therefore, we firmly assert that ***a comprehensive restructuring of Venezuela's public debt is entirely possible.*** Nevertheless, we do not overlook the fact that its implementation will be subject to compliance with a series of essential requirements, leading us to agree with the opinion of numerous experts who warn that, if carried out, its complexity will be extraordinary and exceptional in modern history. Attention to these requirements, and consideration of the inherent challenges, will be fundamental to addressing this process effectively and responsibly.

Before proceeding with specific suggestions for addressing a restructuring or refinancing process for Venezuela's external public debt, we deem it prudent to emphasize, firstly, that this study aims to explore solutions that may have already been proposed in similar terms, as well as to offer interpretations of ideas and theories that may contribute new approaches, seeking to contribute to efforts aimed at ensuring the viability of the restructuring. Secondly, the pressing need to undertake a restructuring leads us to believe that some proposals would be applicable under the current political and economic conditions[130], while others will clearly depend on structural changes in the internal political landscape.

---

[130] When Olivares-Caminal, former UNCTAD advisor on sovereign debt and current advisor to Venezuelan debt creditors, was asked when he considered it appropriate to begin restructuring, he replied, "Right *now, but it should have started yesterday". See:* Olivares-Caminal, Rodrigo, "*Thoughts on the Possible Restructuring of Venezuelan Debt" (interview)*, LEC Abogados, Caracas, 2023.

3.2.2 Essential Guidelines

As KRUEGER -former director of both the World Bank and the IMF- discusses, there is no comprehensive international legal framework establishing an orderly and predictable process for sovereign debt restructuring, nor is there a system guaranteeing the participation of international organizations recognized by both parties. This often complicates the initiation, organization, and systematization of these processes and, in many cases, hinders effective coordination between the various creditors and debtor countries.[131] Therefore, our contribution in this regard will not be based on a strictly personal approach, but rather will focus on establishing a series of ***essential guidelines*** that, by way of example, should be considered by the government in the context of the comprehensive restructuring of Venezuela's external debt.

These guidelines, formulated from a realistic, pragmatic, and strategic perspective in order to achieve an ideal process, are structured as follows:

Guidelines		
	a) Prerequisites	(i) Determination of size and nature (ii) International consensus (iii) National agreement (iv) Transparency and universal consideration of creditors
	b) Strategic	(v) National economic plan (vi) Participation of multilateral organizations (vii) Opening to foreign investment
	c) Structural and institutional	(viii) Adaptation of the legal and regulatory framework (ix) Protection of national assets abroad (x) Restructuring of PDVSA and subsidiaries
	d) Substantive (financial)	(xi) Moratorium (xii) Haircuts (xiii) Reduction of interest rates and extension of terms (siv) Oil-Warrants (xv) Debt conversion (debt-*equity/resource swaps*) * in a separate section

[131] Krueger, Anne, *Op. Cit.*

As can be seen, we assume that debt restructuring will not be a merely technical-financial exercise, as might be assumed in similar cases, but a comprehensive process that requires, as a condition of credibility, a prior and concurrent determination of an economic recomposition strategy capable of sustainably and viably supporting the restructuring.

a) Prerequisites

(i) *Determining the Size and Nature of the Debt*

Given its considerable magnitude and the lack of systematization, it is imperative, before undertaking any process, to conduct a thorough diagnosis of the situation we face. This means identifying the debts the nation is grappling with in order to assess the scope, complexity, and inherent risks of the process. Although it is argued that restructuring should be *comprehensive,* it is essential to consider the different types of liabilities present in order to plan the stages and structure of this extensive process.

On this point, WALKER has considered that the first critical issue to be addressed before initiating this process will be the *identification and assessment of legitimate claims,* followed by the creation of an effective process for dealing with the various creditors in a systematic and consistent manner.[132] Therefore, in agreement with MOATTI and MUCI, we estimate that the first step will necessarily consist of preparing a detailed inventory of the current external public debt, ensuring maximum transparency and adequate coordination between debtor and creditor entities.[133]

As has been mentioned and warned by various advisors and authors, there is concern about the lack of knowledge, even within the government itself, regarding the extent of the debt, the number of creditors, and the nature of each obligation. This significantly complicates the ability to make informed judgments on such a vast issue[134]. Current

132 Walker, Mark, "*Thoughts on the Possible Restructuring of Venezuelan Debt*" (*interview*), *Op. cit.*

133 Moatti, Thomas, and Muci, Frank, *An Economic Framework for Venezuela's Debt Restructuring, Op. cit.*

134 On this matter, Kargman appropriately indicated in 2021 the following: "*Any eventual sovereign debt restructuring promises to be incredibly complex, challenging, and messy.*

estimates calculate that at least US$100 billion corresponds solely to bonds and at least US$15 billion to bilateral debt, but there is no way to know this with certainty[135].

Therefore, it is crucial not only to know the extent of the debt, but also its classification, overdue liabilities, the terms associated with each obligation, and any pending lawsuits. This last aspect is of paramount importance, given that the execution of such lawsuits could further exacerbate the challenges inherent in any restructuring process[136]. The Republic appears to have initiated this phase of the process by conducting an initial assessment of the public sector's external debt, a decision we consider appropriate and a step in the right direction for gaining an initial understanding of the problem[137].

(ii) *International Consensus*

For purely methodological purposes in our study, we will base our analysis on two currently valid premises, which, however, are subject to potential changes: first, that a restructuring process of Venezuela's external public debt must require ***prior negotiation and agreement*** with the United States government and the creditor countries, an aspect we

---

In addition to the sheer size of the debt load that needs to be restructured, there is a huge and widely dispersed creditor body which is likely to make creditor coordination, so critical in restructurings of any scale, a major challenge. There is also a kaleidoscopic array of creditor interests, including bondholders, multilateral development institutions, promissory noteholders, trade creditors/suppliers, arbitration award holders, and claimants to blocked foreign exchange payments. The potentially divergent agendas of these various creditors may well give rise to inter-creditor tensions or conflict ". *Cf.:* Kargman, Steven, "Venezuela: Prospects for Restructuring Sovereign Debt and Rebuilding a National Economy against the backdrop of a Failing State", *Op. cit.*, p. 3.

135 Forbes reported on January 6, 2026, that: "Analysts *estimate that Venezuela currently owes between $150 billion and $170 billion, with JP Morgan calculating that $102 billion of that figure is in bonds, while bilateral debt to China amounts to between $13 billion and $15 billion. Venezuela has not reported debt figures for about a decade, and in the meantime, the state-owned oil company Petróleos de Venezuela (PDVSA) has signed complex oil-backed debt agreements with China.*"

136 According to CEDICE, approximately US$30 billion of Venezuela's sovereign debt (as of 2025) is linked to claims filed with arbitration centers by foreign investors protected by bilateral investment treaties in force with Venezuela. *See:* https://cedice.org.ve/ogp/reporte/deuda-externa-venezolana-demandas-arbitrales/

137 Yapur, Nicolle, "Venezuela, in default, hires Rothschild as debt advisor," in *Bloomberg*, press release of April 23, 2024, available at: https://www.bloomberglinea.com/latinoamerica/venezuela/venezuela-en-default-contrata-a-rothschild-como-asesor-de-deuda/

refer to as "international consensus"; second, that although the economic sanctions imposed by OFAC presuppose a regulatory obstacle to initiating any type of restructuring process[138] (and the idea of a special license for such a broad process has been dismissed on previous occasions),[139] we assume that reaching the aforementioned consensus would entail either the lifting of the economic sanctions or a special *ad hoc license* to carry out this process.

---

[138] "There's *also an OFAC measure against Venezuela issuing new debt - which is necessary to restructure its bonds (workouts are structured as the exchange of old defaulted bonds with new but less valuable ones)". Cf.:* Ferrer, Elías, "Venezuela's long and winding debt restructuring road" in *Financial Times,* Vol. March 2019. Although some authors, such as Humes, have considered that its limitations have always been able to be overcome in relation to bonds and other instruments. The author, who has participated in negotiations as a creditor -- in his role as director of *Geylock Capital* and co-president of the group of Venezuelan creditors, which has opposed the sanctions -- pointed out that: "*These sanctions were poorly designed for the problem it was claimed they were meant to address. The stated purpose of the secondary market trading sanctions was to block the ability (...) to sell bonds to fund their regime. They do not do that. The sanctions prevent US persons from buying bonds in the secondary market, and further specify that any sales must be made to non-US persons only. As a result, the option of selling to a non-US buyer remains if regime-related persons wish to sell. However, if US persons want to sell, or are forced to sell because of a reduction or elimination of Venezuela's index weighting in the EMBI (as was implemented by JP Morgan beginning in July 2019) or due to portfolio redemptions, the buyers will most likely be non-US persons who will almost certainly have interests that are not aligned with the US in how they intend to use the debt that is acquired. The longer the sanctions "If the debt remains in place, the more debt will switch from US hands to these non-US buyers.*" Other authors argued that the negotiation should always have been conducted directly with the US executive branch. Hernández, among others, proposed incorporating the US government into the restructuring process through the *Foreign Claims Settlement Commission* (FCSC) of the Department of Justice. *See*: Hernández, José Ignacio, *The Venezuelan External Public Debt Crisis: Everything Everywhere All at Once,* Center for Strategic and International Studies, March 2023.

[139] On this topic it has been commented: "*There are two requirements that need to be met for debt restructuring to move forward: first, the US Office of Foreign Assets Control (OFAC) would need to issue a license allowing the Venezuelan government to re-enter the primary financial market since a new issuance of bonds must be made for a restructuring. In fact, part of Rothschild's work would be to estimate the possible haircut to be applied, Venezuela's recovery rate, recovery value, oil production, among others while having access to the country's international bank accounts-many of which are currently frozen.*" *Vid.*: Paris, María, "Is Venezuela Headed to Debt Restructuring?" in *Caracas Chronicles,* May 2024. Some authors indicated that nothing could be done in Venezuela other than waiting for a political change that is considered favorable to renegotiate the debt. See generally the comments of: Lowenthal, Abraham F., V *Venezuela's Elusive Transition: Toward a New Path,* Wilson Center, 2021.

On this point, it is worth mentioning that the US Executive issued an Executive Order on January 9, 2026[140] Related to Venezuela's temporary oil production, the US declared a state of emergency to protect all revenues from Venezuelan hydrocarbon activities from embargoes, court-ordered executions, or creditor claims, guaranteeing that these funds are the sovereign property of Venezuela, even though temporarily held by the US Treasury, without implying a "waiver of sovereign immunity." This type of action seems to indicate the possibility of a negotiated restructuring process that would entail lifting the sanctions that originally restricted its initiation and development.

(iii) *Peremptory National Agreement*

Given the above, it seems evident to all analysts of the issue that the possibility of making an international approach to the main creditor governments as well as to multilateral organizations - whose headquarters are either Washington or Brussels - will require a kind of *prior national agreement* between the government and the relevant actors in the national political sphere, with the possible incorporation of civil society.

The idea is to seek a consensus at the national level regarding the need for an opportunity to initiate a restructuring of the public debt, as well as to encourage their eventual participation in the discussion and the manner of carrying out this important process.[141] Fully aware that the current situation is complicated at this point, we cannot fail to bring up this idea, as we consider, after reflection, that it is no longer a mere suggestion, but rather a *prerequisite* for the Venezuelan government.

---

140 Executive Order of the President of the United States of America issued on January 9, 2026: *Safeguarding Venezuelan Oil Revenue for the Good of the American and Venezuelan People. See*: https://www.whitehouse.gov/presidential-actions/2026/01/safeguarding-venezuelan-oil-revenue-for-the-good-of-the-american-and-venezuelan-people/

141 On this point, Rodríguez stated in 2023: "*The way out of Venezuela's current crisis is not through foreign-backed regime change, but through an inclusive political settlement that allows the country's competing factions to coexist. Drawing on the strategies of peace mediation and conflict resolution, negotiations should focus on institutional reforms that make power sharing possible. The United States and its partners should not try to help one side prevail in the fight for control of the state. Rather, they should push the Venezuelan government and opposition to resolve their differences peacefully and cooperate to address the country's problems.*" *Vid.:* Rodríguez, Francisco, "Can Venezuela Chart a Path Out of Crisis?" in *Foreign Affairs,* Vol. Dec, 2023.

Clearly, the legitimacy of this initiative rests on the idea-undoubtedly shared by all-that reorganizing the external debt to protect Venezuela's assets is a matter of *paramount national interest.* For this reason, we must emphasize that the absence of a prior national alliance would hinder a subsequent international agreement with governments, creditors, and multilateral organizations, as it would undermine the process due to a lack of intrinsic legitimacy *from the outset.* This, of course, will be a challenge in itself, one that is beyond the scope of this legal analysis and could be complex enough to jeopardize the very beginning of the comprehensive process of restructuring the national debt.

(iv) *Transparency and Universal Consideration of Creditors*

A successful restructuring must involve as many creditors as possible: the Paris Club (official creditors), the various types of sovereign and PDVSA bondholders, multilateral organizations (IDB, CAF), commercial creditors and, especially, bilateral creditors (the special case of China).

Particularly with regard to financial debt (bonds), the aim would be to prevent *holdout creditors* from hindering the execution of an agreement, as most experts consider them a significant obstacle. In some cases, the *Collective Action Clauses (CACs)* incorporated into the bonds -although, as mentioned, this does not apply to all bond series[142]- would allow a majority of creditors to agree to the restructuring, obligating

142 Buchheit and Gulati warn: "*PDVSA has borrowed in the international bond markets using US-style trust indentures. PDVSA's bonds do not contain collective action clauses (CACs) that would allow a supermajority of holders of a bond to agree to a structuring and thereby bind all holders. That is the bad news. The good news is that the provisions of each series of PDVSA's bonds issued in the international markets under these indentures may be amended with the consent of only a bare majority of holders except for amendments that would: (i) reduce the percentage of holders that must consent to amendments, (ii) reduce the rate of interest or extend the time for payment of interest, (iii) reduce the principal amount payable on the bonds or change the maturity date of the bonds, (iv) change the currency of the bonds, (v) "impair the right of each Holder to receive payment of principal of, premium (if any), interest and Additional Amounts, if any, on such Note on or after the due date thereof or to institute suit to enforce such payment," (vi) subordinate the bonds in right of payment to any other indebtedness, or (vii) change the amendment provisions".* *Vid.*: Buchheit, Lee, and Gulati, Mitu, "How to Restructure Venezuelan Debt", *Op. Cit.*

all creditors to accept the terms, which is essential as an alternative plan. This, however, warrants consideration: given that some sovereign bond issuances-and almost all PDVSA issuances-do not include such Collective Action Clauses (CACs), or require a consensus of 75% or 85% of the bondholders in each series to modify the terms and conditions, a different approach is needed. This approach should seek a *voluntary* and consensual process, presented as an invitation to improve the condition of both the debt and the debtor and creditor, with a view to its sustainability. Otherwise, the viability of restructuring various bond series would be compromised by a lack of agreement and the potential existence of creditors reluctant to participate, as well as creditors who already have favorable rulings.[143] Therefore, it will be necessary not only to secure majority support and control of active lawsuits to avoid protracted legal disputes, but also to ensure *transparency and dialogue* with creditors to build trust and guarantee broad participation.

There is no doubt that Venezuela will need to demonstrate a commitment to its creditors and propose an internal structural reform in order to restore its credibility in international markets.

In any case, we reiterate, the process must include not only large institutional investors, but also small bondholders and bilateral creditors, ensuring that all groups have a voice in the agreement. Certainly, as financial experts indicate, the restructuring must be sequenced and creditor classes prioritized, avoiding premature negotiations with bondholder groups that would increase the risk for strategically important bilateral creditors with whom the debt is already a matter of geopoliti-

143 "*Most sovereign bonds issued today include collective action clauses ("CACs") that allow a super majority of holders across multiple series of bonds to agree to the terms of a restructuring that would be binding on all creditors. Unfortunately, the outstanding bonds of the Republic do not include these modern CACs which allow aggregated voting across series. Two issues of Venezuela's bonds do not contain CACs at all and the balance include CACs that allow holders of 75% (85% in the case of two issues) of the outstanding amount on a series-by-series basis to modify the basic payment and other terms to accommodate the restructuring that Venezuela will require. These are high thresholds and recalcitrant creditors may already have blocking positions in a number of series, or at today's prices (assuming US sanctions permit trading to resume normally) could easily acquire such positions. existing CACs may be sufficient to lock in a restructuring for certain series, it is unlikely that they will prove effective on their own to restructure the Republic's bond debt.*" *Cf.:* Walker, Mark, and Cooper, Richard, *Op. cit.*

cal principle: Russia and China.[144] The reality is that a phased debt negotiation will have to be almost entirely contingent on agreements with those bilateral lenders who could potentially be affected by ongoing negotiations over highly compromised assets.

b) Strategic Guidelines

This section refers to instrumental guidelines for economic reconstruction conceived as prerequisites for the credibility and sustainability of a restructuring process, which must be defined *ex ante* and developed prior to and/or concomitant with the execution of the financial mechanisms.

(v) *National Economic Plan*

The sustainability of any restructuring depends largely on Venezuela's ability to generate long-term revenue, which we presume is possible as a result of an eventual revitalization of the oil industry[145], as well as subsequent economic diversification that guarantees sustained GDP growth.

However, any national reconstruction must begin at least with the outline of a national economic plan for at least the next 10 years, which entails the public and imminent need to carry out reforms aimed at increasing foreign investment from a multi-sectoral point of view (that is, not only concentrated in the oil industry) and improving the country's overall productivity, which may include reforms to the current legal framework to revitalize the national economy, all under the premise of establishing mechanisms for transparency and the proper management of the country's energy resources and PDVSA.

---

144 "*Venezuela has two types of financing with China. One is the long-term US$20 billion fund. The second is the so-called Chinese fund, which comprised an initial US$4 billion and is now worth US$5 billion. The Venezuelan government has sole discrepancy over use of this fund.*" *Cf.:* Dialogue Earth, "China is a long-term player in Venezuela's energy future", available at: https://dialogue.earth/en/energy/6895-china-is-a-long-term-player-in-venezuelas-energy-future/

145 In a report published by Morgan Stanley on January 06, 2026, it was stated: "*A stable government that normalizes relations with the US could unlock significant investment in Venezuela's oil industry, boosting production.*" *See: "Investors Evaluate Developments in Venezuela"*, Morgan Stanley, available at: https://www.morganstanley.com/insights/articles/market-implications-us-intervention-venezuela

According to some authors, Venezuela's economic recovery was considered quite viable in a post-sanction's environment,[146] and it is worth noting that as of the publication date of this study, bonds linked to PDVSA have rebounded, given the change in the country risk outlook reflected by analysts in recent days.[147]

In any case, with this guideline we want to highlight the idea that the Venezuelan government must not only guarantee the generation of income, but must also plan the economic future with a long-term perspective of sustained economic growth, allowing the country to finance its debt without resorting to new defaults (including international monitoring mechanisms that guarantee compliance with the commitments assumed).

(vi) ***Involvement of Multilateral Organizations***

Their inclusion is essential in a process of this magnitude. Certainly, the IMF, the World Bank, and the IDB would play a key role in the restructuring, providing technical assistance and lending credibility to the process, as well as, if necessary, through concessional financing programs or credit facilities to stabilize finances and, at the same time, ensure the possibility of repayment. Furthermore, it would be inconsistent to seek external financing through bonds issued in New York while simultaneously evading the advice of the IMF or the IDB, institutions in which those same creditors rely to coordinate a repayment process.

---

146 It has been commented on this: "*Venezuela's macroeconomic fundamentals look strong compared with other countries in default. In Argentina, entrenched popular ill-will toward bailout conditions imposed by the International Monetary Fund (IMF) have hampered debt negotiations for decades. In crisis-stricken Lebanon, the government has racked up debt equivalent to 150% of national output with few viable economic options for repayment. Venezuela's natural resources endowment, which includes gold, iron ore and other commodities in addition to oil, means that the country has a clear path to solvency. Since Chevron summarized its exports from Venezuela, its oil production there has grown rapidly to 100,000 barrels per day. That figure is expected to double by 2025, by which time the oil major will have recovered the $3 billion owed to it by Caracas. Cf.:* Youkee, Mat, "Venezuela Sovereign Debt: A Hefty Wager", in *LatinFinance,* Jul. 2023.

147 Morgan Stanley stated in a report dated January 06, 2026: "*The debt market is likely to see more immediate effects from recent events, with bonds of the government of Venezuela and the state-controlled oil producer PDVSA continuing their rally after strong gains in late 2025.*" *Op. cit.*

This, it should be noted, is more pragmatic than ideological, and the nation has little chance of dispensing with their participation.[148]

(vii) *Flexible Foreign Investment Outlook*

For the restructuring to be sustainable, Venezuela must function as a hub for foreign investment, not only in the hydrocarbons sector (through new oil fields within the current framework) but also in other sectors of international interest: electricity, mining, agriculture, tourism, and so on. Again, the realistic capacity to meet the new commitments will require innovative solutions that provide financial security to creditors while simultaneously fostering the growth of the national economy. This process should be used to relaunch the country on the international stage, allowing Venezuela to begin its path toward restoring credibility in international markets.

The recovery of the oil industry, whether through traditional methods (infrastructure, production) or more unorthodox approaches (mixed service models with international companies), has already been discussed in the international market, despite its cost and complexity. The implementation of a comprehensive plan to open the sector to foreign investment, following the revitalization of the oil industry and the restoration of legal certainty, is foreseeable. Therefore, we do not see this as a challenge in terms of its certainty, but rather in terms of its proper execution.

c) Structural and Institutional Guidelines

This section refers to structural or institutional guidelines that make the restructuring functional, that is, that it can be implemented in practice with the greatest possible willingness to achieve its goal.

---

148 "*The participation of the International Monetary Fund, the World Bank, or the Inter-American Development Bank in the Venezuelan case provides the necessary technical support for negotiations with creditors. Furthermore, the presence of these organizations enhances the credibility of the process, increasing the participation of a greater number of creditors.*" *Cf.*: Carrasquero, Andrés; Escovar, Ramón; Campos, Mariana; and Freitas, Víctor, *Op. Cit.*, p. 39.

(viii) *Adjustment of the Legal and Regulatory Framework*

At this point, we agree with most authors who indicate that, under the current regulatory framework, the nation could be hindered from initiating and participating in a process of this magnitude with the necessary flexibility, given the diversity of creditors and debts assumed. A position, already discussed, calls for the creation of a modern insolvency regulatory framework aligned with both international practices and international bankruptcy laws, which could be applicable to public entities such as PDVSA. PDVSA's status as a functionally decentralized public administration entity casts doubt on the application of even the Venezuelan Commercial Code, let alone subjecting it to foreign insolvency laws.[149]

Within this legal framework, modifications could be considered in the following regulatory frameworks:

---

[149] On this matter, Italiani *et al have commented: "There are two insolvency procedures under Venezuelan law: (1) the moratorium process; and (2) the bankruptcy process. Although the regime may be used either to liquidate business enterprises or to reorganize them, recent practice seems to show that if a company is salvageable, most stakeholders prefer to have an out-of-court restructuring. The Venezuelan bankruptcy process is seen as vexatious, reflecting in part the fact that there is still a social stigma attached to businesses that go bankrupt. There is much speculation as to whether Venezuelan public entities can be subject to the Code of Commerce's insolvency regimes. PDVSA and its subsidiaries in Venezuela are organized as public limited companies under the Code of Commerce and logic would dictate that the Code's bankruptcy provisions should apply to them. and gas distribution infrastructure located in Venezuela, must be automatically stayed for 45 days while the Ministry of Energy and Petroleum deploys a plan that will ensure the uninterrupted supply of oil, derivatives and gas to the market. This protection from attachments and provisional remedies has been considered by scholars as a type of immunity that would complicate the application of the bankruptcy regime of the Code of Commerce to PDVSA, as a significant portion of the national oil company's most valuable operational assets may fall outside the reach of compulsory liquidation proceedings. Some might say that PDVSA's insolvency would require the procedural rules currently in effect in Venezuela to be adapted to take account of the underlying public policy issues involved to avoid affecting the provision of a public service of general interest. Other legal commentators have taken a different view. Neither position has been tested in the Venezuelan courts in relation to the oil and gas industry.[15] If the bankruptcy regime of the Code of Commerce were to be considered not to be applicable to PDVSA by the competent court, which in our view would be the Venezuelan Supreme Tribunal, there would be no another specific set of rules that would regulate PDVSA's insolvency or its liquidation."* *Cf.:* Italiani, Fulvio; Omaña, Carlos; and Pettersson, Roland, *Op. cit.*

(i) **LOAF:** a reform to the current LOAF in matters pertaining to the range of operations that may include restructuring and the possibility of considering initiatives from both the National Assembly, the Executive and even the decentralized entities themselves, which would be subject to the same legal requirements but would accept greater flexibility.

(ii) **Special Law:** The enactment of a *special law for the restructuring of external public debt* that would allow, as occurred in the refinancings of 1985 and 1990, the use of dynamic and creative negotiation mechanisms. Furthermore, at this point, the possibility of creating a *national debt committee could be considered,* with the authority to address the process comprehensively and with a comprehensive and temporary organizational structure that would allow for the centralization of the entire process in relation to international creditors and multilateral organizations.

(iii) **Legal regime of hydrocarbons:** reform of the legal framework governing the exploration and exploitation of hydrocarbons and the participation of foreign investment in joint ventures created with the purpose of contemplating, at least, the exchange of debt for exploitation rights and other similar mechanisms.

(iv) **Commercial Code:** provisions of the Commercial Code in relation to insolvency proceedings and the classification of liabilities of decentralized entities.

(v) **Fiscal matters:** tax reforms that guarantee greater transparency and accountability in the management of public finances.

This is only a preliminary and illustrative list of aspects that could be taken into account in a possible reform of the legal regime of restructuring, a topic that deserves a genuine doctrinal discussion, since it would be senseless for the start of a process of this magnitude to be restricted by orthodox rules more suited to the normal functioning of public finances than to extraordinary processes such as the one analyzed.

(ix) *Protection of National Assets*

A critical point in the overall restructuring, which would certainly include the claims on PDVSA's guaranteed bonds, would be ensuring that strategic assets, such as *Citgo* and its refineries, are not subject to seizure or judicial execution by creditors, which would torpedo the process from the outset.[150] Without going into the details of *how to achieve this* (since there are multiple, even conflicting, positions on this-some traditional, others unorthodox, and still others pragmatic), it will always be a key condition for a successful restructuring.

On this point, the experience of asset protection measures against creditors implemented during *Iraq 's debt restructuring* (2003-2005), led by the United Nations Security Council and the United States, is relevant. While there are arguments in favor (BUCHHEIT and GULATI), there are also critical positions (WALKER) regarding the application of such measures to PDVSA, based on the argument that they could affect its credibility with foreign investors. Considering the current situation, the pressure from creditors, and the vulnerability of assets abroad, we believe that these protective measures are a pragmatic way to safeguard national assets, without prejudice to considering other mechanisms that have the same objective but operate differently.

(x) *Reorganization of PDVSA and Subsidiaries*

We must point out that, to date, we do not consider the possibility of liquidating PDVSA, as suggested by many authors, especially international ones, to be advisable for several reasons.[151] Firstly, because

---

[150] On this point, Walker and Cooper correctly indicated the following: "*The most critical and time-sensitive task is to normalize the status of PDVSA and protect its assets and operations, notwithstanding the fact that total claims against the Republic exceed those against PDVSA. Venezuela's future recovery and its ability to generate hard currency are and will remain for a long time heavily dependent on the country's ability to exploit its abundant oil and gas reserves. And although the role of PDVSA going forward may change dramatically as substantial private capital is committed to the oil and gas industry and Venezuela relies more on royalties and income taxes than on proceeds from exports by PDVSA itself, PDVSA is nevertheless likely to continue to play an important role in this critical sector of the economy. Thus, safeguarding the assets of PDVSA outside Venezuela-both tangible assets like Citgo as well as accounts receivable-and its ability to conduct business around the world are of paramount importance and will be essential to its ability to new capital and strategic partners.*" *Cf.:* Walker, Mark, and Cooper, Richard, *Op. cit.*

[151] Proposals by Buchheit and Gulati, but also Pettersson and later Italiani *et al.*

the legal framework applicable to this company is, as has been stated, predominantly public law, making it unfeasible to subject it to a process governed exclusively by private law in a foreign jurisdiction, such as *Chapter 15 bankruptcy proceedings* -or any other private law procedure[152]-although this is entirely possible for other authors, either under the current legal framework[153] or through the creation of a special law for PDVSA.[154] Secondly, even if it were possible, and assuming the applicable framework were strictly private law and governed by the Commercial Code, we believe that the national importance of this decentralized entity is such that considering liquidation to benefit creditors might seem like a rash suggestion for the government, regardless of its potential benefits.

In this regard, we believe it is more appropriate to evaluate the idea of a corporate reorganization, that is, a modification of its corporate structure. Indeed, a more moderate and suitable possibility might be to create a new state-owned company, distinct from PDVSA (but a subsidiary of this *holding company)*, as suggested by LEVIN and PETTERSSON in 2019.[155]

---

152 Zandstra points out that there are precedent cases where a state-owned company has been subjected, extraordinarily, to bankruptcy processes similar to Chapter 15: "*There are successful instances where a state-owned corporation originally not subject to a functioning bankruptcy / re-organization regime has become the subject of a new functioning such regime as a precursor to restructuring its debt obligations. Dubai World is a relatively recent example*". *Vine.:* Zandstra, Deborah, *Op. cit.*

153 Levin and Pettersson maintain: "*PDVSA is an SOE adopting the form of a corporation (public limited company). As such it is subject to a Private Law framework, given that they are created using legal forms consistent with Commercial Law, regardless of the involvement of the State in their inception or the existence of public funding in the form of equity, notwithstanding their hybrid public-private nature and consequential applicability of special rules of public or administrative law.*" *Op. cit.*

154 Walker points out that: "*The first step would be for Venezuela to enact a new law that would enable PDVSA to restructure its liabilities through a process that is consistent with Chapter 15 of the US Bankruptcy code. The new law would be administered by a special court to be established with newly appointed independent judges. PDVSA and its creditors (all of them, not just bondholders, but separated into different classes if and to the extent appropriate) would then seek to negotiate a consensual restructuring.*" *Cf.:* Walker, Mark, *Op. cit.*

155 "*Indeed, the rather generic reference of Article 27 of the Hydrocarbons Organic Act seems to confirm the constitutional possibility of having the Venezuelan State create a new SOE 'for the management of the oil industry,' thus replacing PDVSA in its current role as Venezuelan' oil industry operator.*" *Vine.:* Levin, Richard, and Pettersson, Roland, *Op. cit.*

The idea here is that this corporate reorganization allows for a partial subrogation of certain rights linked to the primary activities of exploration and exploitation, to hold hydrocarbon licenses simultaneously with PDVSA and other subsidiaries, but to be able to assume, totally or partially, the responsibility for certain sovereign debt liabilities, committing to the payment of the bonds charged to oil revenues.

This would certainly require the review and modification of the current hydrocarbon legal framework in Venezuela and, surely, special laws that incorporate insolvency principles applied in the private sector, as has happened in comparative law with other state-owned companies that required *ad hoc regulations* to guarantee their restructuring or orderly liquidation.[156]

d) Substantive (Financial) Guidelines

This section of the issue is properly a matter of financial engineering and, again, goes beyond legal considerations. We will simply suggest that a restructuring process such as the one anticipated must necessarily be as flexible and innovative as legally possible, adapting to the needs of the current financial landscape. Regarding the restructuring of financial debt, we acknowledge that it will vary depending on whether the obligations are derived from *Sovereign Bonds* or *PDVSA Bonds,* as both have different applicable conditions and procedures, making it essential to address each separately.

Regarding the substantive particularities from a financial point of view, assuming the comprehensiveness of a restructuring process, we believe that the essential thing would be to consider the origin of a range of traditional options used in similar situations, as well as heterodox

156 We can highlight the case of the Croatian agricultural conglomerate *Agrokor,* which, despite being a private company subject to a special regime of strategic protection by the Croatian state, filed for *Chapter 15 bankruptcy protection* in New York. This protracted process culminated in an agreement with American creditors and the creation of a new local company. *See*: Clarke, Ben, "*Agrokor granted Chapter 15 protection in New York*", in *Global Restructuring Review,* September 24, 2018, available at: https://globalrestructuringreview.com/article/agrokor-granted-chapter-15-protection-in-new-york ; and Rancic, Nedad, "Agrokor. A case of controlled collapse," in Beros, Recker *et al., Economic and Social Development: 27th International Scientific Conference on Economic and Social Development,* Croatia, 2018, pp. 753–762.

alternatives that provide flexibility without losing credibility, among which we highlight the following:

(xi) *Moratorium*

A debt payment moratorium (also known as a *standstill)* involves the temporary suspension of debt service payments-principal, interest, or both-for an agreed period, without, in principle, implying a nominal reduction of the debt. Its purpose is to alleviate the debtor's liquidity pressure by freezing a potential initial default while macroeconomic conditions are established that allow for the reestablishment of a sustainable payment schedule.

It is clear that by not servicing the debt, there is a *de facto moratorium* on payment obligations. However, we are referring here to a *negotiated standstill,* that is, one agreed upon and negotiated with creditors and legally structured. Under this scenario, it would be desirable for Venezuela to negotiate such a grace period to suspend certain significant payments (interest and/or principal), with the express purpose of facilitating the initial recovery of the country's productive sector and its macroeconomic stabilization.

While it has been said that moratoria are often perceived as a sign of financial weakness on the part of the debtor that can affect the confidence of creditors, studies in the private sector related to commercial debt have shown that moratoria can be beneficial for the parties involved, insofar as they improve repayment in the medium term and contribute to long-term sustainability, especially in complex insolvency environments.[157]

In the case of Venezuela, it is evident that the country would need a post-restructuring moratorium to reactivate the oil industry while simultaneously revitalizing other strategic economic sectors and internally reorganizing the distribution of oil, tax, and parafiscal revenues. However, for this to be viable and acceptable to creditors, it must necessarily be integrated into a comprehensive economic plan, agreed upon and credible by the creditors. Indeed, the moratorium only postpones potential insolvency (it does not resolve it), so its effectiveness depends

[157] Fiorin, Stefano; Hall, Joseph; and Kanz, Martin, "How Do Borrowers Respond to a Debt Moratorium?: Experimental Evidence from Consumer Loans in India", WorldBank Group, 2023.

on its coordination with other complementary measures (other classic mechanisms analyzed later), which, in our proposal, would include all the measures and objectives of the aforementioned "national economic plan," which would also be aligned with the "international consensus" previously reached for the development of the restructuring process.

This ideal starting condition for the debt restructuring process will likely be tested during the negotiation phase, as it may not be fully accepted by the large group of creditors whose claims have been delayed for years and who face an understandable urgency to begin receiving payments that provide certainty to their financial situation.

(xii) *Haircuts*

The moratorium would operate as a temporary liquidity relief strategy, but not as a permanent debt adjustment mechanism to make repayment sustainable in a post-restructuring scenario. For that, nominal debt reductions or "*haircuts*" would need to be negotiated. Indeed, we believe that this complementary measure is imperative in applicable cases, as the magnitude of Venezuela's debt warrants such reductions.

A haircut implies a direct reduction of the principal owed. From a pragmatic standpoint, it would be natural to expect the country to propose nominal haircuts *from the outset* - that is, a considerable reduction of a few percentage points in its liabilities to alleviate the financial burden and make it sustainable, as has occurred in all recent restructurings: Argentina, Iraq, Greece, among others, where significant haircuts ranging from 60% to 80% were negotiated. While we cannot anticipate the magnitude of these haircuts, most authors who have analyzed Venezuela's external debt consider them necessary.

As KARGMAN POINTED OUT in 2020, analyzing a potential restructuring of Venezuelan debt, "it *might be necessary for Venezuela's creditors to forgive some of the debt -i.e., reductions in the principal of certain existing debt obligations, also known as 'haircuts'- in order for Venezuela to be left with a sustainable debt burden after the restructuring.*"[158]

However, the different categories of creditors suggest different restructuring conditions. It has been mentioned, for example, that although

[158] Kargman, Steven, "Venezuela's Potential Debt Restructuring and Economic Recovery Efforts: Some Key Legal and Policy Challenges," *Op. Cit.*

the *Paris Club* has occasionally offered debt relief through write-offs, its predominant approach is "*rescheduling*", that is, the rescheduling of payments (deferrals, staggered approaches), which could exempt them from nominal write-offs. This can lead, as OLIVARES-CAMINAL points out, to the existence of different categories of financial debt: bonds whose restructuring involves significant write-offs and others that are honored at their full value, as happened in the Greek restructuring.[159]

This matter, once again, requires prior discussion and negotiation of discounts to the nominal value of the debt based on realistic payments that are sustainable in medium- and long-term projections for creditors. This will depend on many variables and how these haircuts or reductions are structured. Large *haircuts* will make the debt more sustainable but will be more difficult to negotiate, while small *haircuts* will be more acceptable but will carry the risk of eventual default if the reduction is not adequate for the realistic payment projections. Furthermore, all negotiations must take into account potential losses for creditors and the country's outlook from the perspective of foreign investment.[160]

(xiii) *Reduction of Interest Rates and Extension of Maturity Dates*

These complementary mechanisms would basically be economic *haircuts,* which are indispensable since the restructuring will hardly involve refinancing the bonds by reducing rates to have manageable interest or extending maturity dates to reduce short-term pressure on public finances.

---

159 The author commented: "*However, when restructuring each bond separately, not reaching the majority in one issue will result in that bond not being restructured through the use of CACs. This might create two categories of bonds, those being restructured and accepting a hefty haircut and others that are not. This happened in Greece where some bonds received a 53.5% haircut and others were honored at full face value*". *Vine.:* Olivares-Caminal, Rodrigo, "Thoughts on the Possible Restructuring of Venezuelan Debt" (interview), *Op. cit.*

160 As they point out Sturzenegger and Zettelmeyer, "*On the one hand, a debt restructuring that is perceived as letting private creditors off too easily may raise concerns about "investor moral hazard", if it occurs in the context of official crisis lending or official debt forgiveness (...). On the other hand, a restructuring that involves high investor losses may raise concerns about debtor moral hazard, and the future of the sovereign debt market. Cf.* : Sturzenegger, Federico; Zettelmeyer, Jeromin, "Haircuts: Estimating investor losses in sovereign debt restructurings, 1998–2005, in Journal of International Money and Finance, Vol. 27(5), September 2008.

This presents a challenge that has been overcome in previous cases, as WALKER and COOPER, who have studied a potential restructuring in Venezuela, point out, indicating that "*historically, sovereigns that have faced a similar mix of debt (unsecured bonds, bilateral debt, claims and arbitration awards and litigation) have managed to restructure the vast majority of their debt using traditional techniques and have succeeded in protecting their critical assets located outside their borders.*"[161]

For certain authors, regardless of the political reality, both assumptions have always been necessary to resolve Venezuela's external debt crisis. Indeed, BUCHHEIT and GULATI, authors familiar with Greek debt and the Venezuelan case in some detail, have indicated that the question will be "*what level of debt the country can bear assuming a rigorous economic adjustment program and renewed support from the international community*", both of which we consider certain should this process take place. They maintain that: "*For these reasons, the restructuring may not initially require significant reductions in the principal. Undoubtedly, Venezuela will not be able to allocate much money to debt service while it tries to overcome its current situation. Therefore, in the first phase, an extension of maturities along with a sharp reduction in coupons will be necessary. At the end of this extension period (say, five years), a judgment can be made as to whether a more lasting debt restructuring is needed and, if so, what the terms of that restructuring would be.*"[162]

(xiv) *Oil-Warrants*

The term *"oil warrants,"* used in post-default external debt restructuring literature, refers to a type of contingency clause that links payments and benefits to creditors directly to the performance of the debtor country's oil industry. Thus, they are not strictly financial *warrants* (like *commodity reference warrants or CoRWs,* which are negotiable structured instruments), but rather functional incentives for creditors seeking to offset nominal or economic *haircuts* and providing the possibility of *upside sharing* between the country and creditors when oil prices rise.

The proposal to incorporate *oil warrants* into potential restructuring negotiations was made, among others, by MOATTI and MUCI in a

[161] *Cf.:* Walker, Mark, and Cooper, Richard, *Op. cit.*

[162] *Vid.*: Buchheit, Lee, and Gulati, Mitu, "How to Restructure Venezuelan Debt", *Op. Cit.*

2019 document that analyzed the possibility of restructuring Venezuelan debt, in which they point out as a general recommendation "*to make value recovery instruments ("oil warrants") a central instrument in the debt restructuring strategy to manage oil price uncertainty and avoid repeated pressures on the balance of payments in the event of lower oil prices.*"[163]

The authors further add that, given that any projected balance of payments for Venezuela will be extremely sensitive to oil prices and oil production, a situation of uncertainty for creditors will be inevitable in a scenario of falling prices. Therefore, they argue that, in that scenario, Venezuela "could *face heightened balance of payments pressures and could be forced into a new restructuring after a few months or years, jeopardizing the recovery*". For this reason, "oil *warrants should be a critical component of the negotiation to compensate for the high nominal and market cuts if oil prices rise* [which] *would ensure that the government shares the benefits of higher oil prices and production with creditors, while limiting the creditors' potential benefit to a reasonable level.*"[164]

As KARGMAN, who has also commented on this mechanism, points out, "if *the price of oil exceeds a predetermined baseline projection, creditors will be entitled to an additional payment, beyond the debt service payments they would otherwise receive under the terms of the restructured debt. Therefore, if the baseline oil price projection turns out to be too conservative, creditors can obtain an additional benefit based on a better-than-expected oil price.*"[165] It is for this reason that the author views the incorporation of this mechanism not so much as a necessity, but rather as an incentive for creditors.

3.2.3. Regarding the possibility of converting debt into equity

We analyze this point separately because, more than a heterodox financial restructuring tool, it is a mechanism that involves a legal pro-

---

163 Moatti, Thomas, and Muci, Frank, *An Economic Framework for Venezuela's Debt Restructuring, Op. cit.*

164 *Idem.*

165 Kargman, Steven, "*Thoughts on the Possible Restructuring of Venezuelan Debt*" (*interview), Op. cit.*

posal with significant economic, regulatory, and political implications, which go beyond those posed by the traditional mechanisms discussed, which will undoubtedly be applied in our restructuring without major complexities.

Indeed, the possibility of implementing debt swaps or conversions, proposed by various national and foreign authors, requires its own analysis linked to its operability and legal basis within the present and future regulatory framework.

a) Debt-Equity Swaps

This mechanism proposes the conversion of sovereign debt into equity participation in public companies. In its concrete implementation, the debt *swap could be carried out* with participation in public, mixed companies and even for rights to exploit resources, directly or through vehicles designed for this purpose.[166]

(i) *Background*

These conversion mechanisms originated in the early 1980s, stemming from defaults in developing economies. They emerged more as a financial innovation than as a policy of multilateral organizations[167], although the IMF later adopted them, and they experienced significant growth until the early 1990s.[168] In Latin America, this type of conversion was successfully used in *Chile* (1985) and *Brazil* (1989), as well as in Argentina and, to a lesser extent, in Bolivia, Peru, Ecuador, and Mexico,[169] the latter as complementary mechanisms within the *Brady Plan.* It is worth noting that these economies were, for the most part,

[166] On the subject see in general: Edwards, Sebastian, *Capital Flows, Foreign Direct Investment and Debt-equity swaps in developing countries,* National Bureau of Economic Research, 1990; Grosse, Robert, "The Debt/Equity Swap in Latin America- In Whose Interest?" in *Journal of International Financial Management and Accounting,* Vol. 4(1), March 1992.

[167] Ganitsky, Joseph; and Lema, Gerardo; "Foreign Investment Through Debt-Equity Swaps," in *MIT Sloan Management Review*; Cambridge Vol. 29(2), Winter 1998.

[168] In addition to Latin America, this mechanism was applied in Eastern Europe (Poland, Hungary, Romania), in Asia (Philippines, Indonesia) and Africa (Nigeria and Egypt).

[169] For an analysis of the application of *debt-equity swaps* in Latin America, see the study: Blackwell, Michael and Nocera, Simon, "Debt-Equity Swaps", in Frenkel, Jacob, Dooley, Michael, et al., *Analytical issues in debt,* IMF, 1989.

transitioning to privatization schemes, which facilitated access to foreign direct investment in pre-default situations.[170] However, we observe that by the mid-1990s, the mechanism declined due to macroeconomic stabilization efforts that favored foreign direct investment mechanisms.

(ii) *Operability*

The benefit envisioned with these types of *swaps* was to reduce debt while simultaneously attracting foreign investment by converting a financial obligation into an economic share of risk. As WALLENSTEIN points out this share traditionally involves privatization, which can be achieved through investment in the stock market or direct investment.[171] In all cases, this mechanism requires a clear and defined regulatory framework, as well as a national economic and political commitment. Given that it represents a form of privatization and has been used in strategic sectors, its viability demands not only comprehensive regulatory reform but also a long-term strategic economic plan.

(iii) *Considerations on its applicability in Venezuela's Debt Restructuring*

According to ZANDSTRA, who has closely studied the Venezuelan case, *debt-equity programs, stemming from the Brady Plan* era, could represent the greatest contribution to reducing Venezuelan sovereign debt during the restructuring.[172] However, this aspect warrants further examination because, although it technically exceeds the scope of this study, such proposals imply the potential participation of third parties in hydrocarbon projects through companies in the oil sector, which, in our case, are state-owned enterprises and, as such, functionally decentralized entities that form part of the public patrimony.

---

170 Edwards, Sebastian, *Op. Cit.*

171 "*The debt-equity swap is a mechanism by which a bank exchanges foreign sovereign external debt of a debtor country for an equity stake in a company in that country through privatization, stock market investment, or direct investment. That is, a bank holding debt has three choices. It can (1) continue to hold the debt, (2) try to sell it in the secondary market, or (3) swap it, either for debt of another country or for an equity stake*". *Cf.:* Wallenstein, Stephen, "Debt-Equity Swaps and Conversion Funds", in Effros, Robert, *Current Legal Issues Affecting Central Banks,* Vol. II, IMF, 1994.

172 The author is part of Clifford Chance and has issued documents and participated in forums on Venezuelan sovereign debt. Zandstra, Deborah, *Op. Cit.*

Within the current constitutional and legal framework in Venezuela for the oil industry, an operation of this nature could not be carried out without a comprehensive modification of that legal regime and, assuming that this were carried out, the operability of this mechanism would have to be evaluated beforehand with respect to PDVSA and its subsidiaries from an operational point of view, admitting a flexibility hitherto unheard of in our administrative organization.

Having said that, there is a precedent for exchanging Venezuelan external debt for shares in a company, but we note that the factual and particular conditions of that transaction make it difficult for it to properly constitute a precedent. Indeed, although it was a bond-for-equity swap, the exchange appears very different from those involving foreign participation in Venezuelan oil companies (which are the ones proposed by the doctrine), since it was carried out on assets abroad that were acquired by PDVSA, through an *ad hoc subsidiary* (PDV *Caribe, SA)*, within the framework of the *Petrocaribe Agreement* for the sale of crude oil between Venezuela and the Dominican Republic. The transaction, however, was beneficial for both parties and revealed the advisability of exploring novel restructuring alternatives and allowed for testing OFAC's acceptance of such mechanisms.[173]

The *swap* in question was carried out in 2021, when a Dominican business group (Patsa *Ltd.)* A holder of *defaulted PDVSA bonds* negotiated to receive, as payment for its bonds, 49% of the shares of PDV Caribe, SA (PDVSA) in the state-owned oil company *Refinería Dominicana de Petróleo, SA* (Refidomsa*)*, which Venezuela had acquired due to the Dominican state's failure to pay for crude oil shipments. The exchange, organized to include the participation of interested parties and the government of the Dominican Republic (which ultimately acquired these shares from Patsa Ltd.), was accepted by OFAC and allowed Venezuela to liquidate its *defaulted bonds* (at a 74.5% discount) and *Refidomsa* to change ownership to become a wholly state-owned company, thus exempting it from the limitations of the economic sanctions that had applied to it due to PDVSA's previous equity stake.[174]

[173] Carrasquero, Andrés; Escovar, Ramón; and Campos, Mariana, *Op. cit.*

[174] Press release from the Ministry of Finance of the Dominican Republic dated August 19, 2021, entitled "*Dominican Government Acquires Control of 100% of Refidomsa Shares,*"

b) *Debt-Resource Swaps: Conversion of Debt into Oil & Gas Projects*

Instead of considering a *debt-equity* In addition to traditional *swaps,* which seek equity participation in mixed public companies, we project an oil opening plan in which debt-resource swaps are carried out, *where the* total or partial conversion of sovereign bonds is linked to exploitation rights in hydrocarbon projects through allocations, without this representing direct participation of the creditors in State companies.

As KARGMAN indicated, it would not be a classic debt-for-equity swap, but rather an exchange of bonds for "*oil development rights granted to the creditor participating in the restructuring*", adding that "*for creditors who choose to take advantage of this debt-for-equity swap, they would be betting on a possible benefit if they successfully develop the reserves allocated to them and if, for example, the price of oil rises beyond current expectations.*"[175]

Even in a scenario of openness, we recognize that this is not an easy proposal to implement, among other things because oil and industry have always been considered part of national sovereignty and closely linked to the economic security of Venezuelans. However, the current situation warrants its study, given that, in one way or another, national reconstruction is tied to the oil industry, and any consensus that Venezuela may reach with international creditors will necessarily imply an opening of the hydrocarbon sector as an anchor for generating income through foreign investment. The deterioration of the infrastructure is such that it could hardly be carried out without the assistance, sought or not, of the large transnational oil companies.

A project of this nature will require a delicate balance between sustainability, sovereignty, credibility, and pragmatism, something that will undoubtedly be challenging in the Venezuelan case.

---

available at: https://www.hacienda.gob.do/gobierno-dominicano-adquiere-el-control-del-100-de-las-acciones-de-refidomsa/

175 Kargman, Steven, "Thoughts *on the Possible Restructuring of Venezuelan Debt"* (interview*), Op. cit.*

IV. CONCLUSIONS

1. The comprehensive restructuring of Venezuela's external public debt is an essential and priority condition for the country's economic and institutional reconstruction in the short and medium term. A serious planning process for this restructuring must be urgently initiated, both because of the magnitude of the external debt-which could exceed US$175 billion-and because of the restrictive nature of this problem for any economic recovery strategy. The pressure from creditors, the state of the national patrimony, and the direct impact of public finance management on the Venezuelan population make it impossible to postpone the national academic debate on this immediate challenge.
2. While the current state of Venezuela's external public debt presents unprecedented characteristics, it is not foreign to Venezuela's financial history. External debt and its successive refinancing and restructuring processes have been a constant since the Republic's inception, and a historical overview not only reveals a record of recurring crises but also offers relevant lessons about the risks of excessive dependence on oil revenues and the need for fiscal and institutional discipline. In this sense, the indebtedness of recent decades appears more as a consequence of the mismanagement of extraordinary resources than as a strictly circumstantial phenomenon.
3. Doctrinal, regulatory, and comparative analysis reveals that, despite numerous legal, political, and operational obstacles, there is no material or legal impossibility that precludes the viability of a comprehensive restructuring of Venezuela's sovereign debt. On the contrary, such a process is entirely feasible, although foreseeably extraordinary in its complexity and unprecedented in contemporary practice. Its success will depend on compliance with a series of essential conditions and on a technically rigorous, transparent, and coordinated implementation at both the domestic and international levels.
4. Given that there is no single or predetermined mechanism in international law for sovereign debt restructuring, and considering the unique nature of the Venezuelan case, this study proposes a series

of general, non-exhaustive guidelines that should guide any future restructuring process:

(i) Minimum Prerequisites:
   a. Determination of magnitude and nature.
   b. International consensus.
   c. peremptory national agreement.
   d. Transparency and universal consideration of creditors.

(ii) Strategic Guidelines for Economic Policy:
   a. National economic plan.
   b. Participation of multilateral organizations.
   c. Opening up to foreign investment.

(iii) Structural and Institutional Guidelines:
   a. Adaptation of the legal and regulatory framework.
   b. Protection of national assets abroad.
   c. Restructuring of PDVSA and subsidiaries.

(iv) Substantive Financial Guidelines:
   a. Moratorium.
   b. Haircuts.
   c. Reduction of interest rates and extension of terms.
   d. Oil-Warrants.
   e. Debt Conversion (*debt-equity/resource swaps)*.

5. In particular, regarding the debt conversion mechanism, it is proposed that it not be limited to traditional *debt-equity swaps, but could be structured using debt-resource swaps* (DRS) for the exploitation of natural resources in the hydrocarbons sector. This approach would link the resolution of external debt with productive reactivation, without necessarily implying direct equity participation by creditors in state-owned enterprises, thus preserving the traditional administrative organization and sovereignty over the control of natural resources.
6. An orderly and strategically articulated restructuring of external public debt can become not only an instrument of financial sustainability, but a central axis for channeling productive investment, revitalizing the oil industry and laying the foundations for a lasting economic reconstruction for Venezuela.

V. REFERENCES

Acemoglu, Daron, "The Great Debt Cleanup" (June 23, 2020), in *Project Syndicate,* New York, 2020, available at: https://www.project-syndicate.org/commentary/plan-to-navigate-emerging-market-debts-by-daron-acemoglu-2020-06

Alayón, Ángel, "Venezuela: External Debt in Figures", *Prodavinci,* Caracas, 2017, available at: https://especiales.prodavinci.com/deudaexterna/

Badell Madrid, Rafael, "Comments on Judgment No. 821 of the Political-Administrative Chamber of the Supreme Tribunal of Justice dated December 8, 2022, referring to contracts of national public interest", in *Revista de Derecho Público,* No. 171-172, Editorial Jurídica Venezolana, Caracas, 2022, p. 319, available at: https://revistadederechopublico.com/archivos/revistas/revista-de-derecho-publico-director-no-171-172-julio-diciembre-2022

Badell Madrid, Rafael, "Contracts *of National Public Interest",* in *Revista de Derecho Administrativo,* No. 19, July-December 2004, Caracas, 2004, available at: http://www.ulpiano.org.ve/revistas/bases/artic/texto/RDA/19/rda_2004_19_41-67.pdf

Badell Madrid, Rafael, "Contracts of Public Interest" in *Public Law Review,* No. 159-160, Venezuelan Legal Publishing House, Caracas, 2021, available at: https://badellgrau.com/revista-de-derecho-publico-nro-159-160/

Banking and Business, "Torino: Venezuelan external debt represents 186% of GDP" (May 6, 2019), Caracas, 2019, available at: https://www.bancaynegocios.com/torino-deuda-externa-venezolana-representa-186-del-pib/

Berglund, Susan, "The Public Debt of Venezuela: Causes and Effects, 1830-1870", in Liehr, Reinhard, *The public debt in Latin America in historical perspective,* Bibliotheca Ibero-Americana Vervuert, Madrid, 1995, p. 421, available at: https://publications.iai.spk-berlin.de/servlets/MCRFileNodeServlet/Document_derivate_00002004/BIA_058_417_445.pdf

Blackwell, Michael and Nocera, Simon, "Debt-Equity Swaps", in Frenkel, Jacob, Dooley, Michael, et al., *Analytical issues in debt,* International Monetary Fund, 1989.

Borensztein, Eduardo and Panizza, Ugo, *The Costs of Sovereign Debt Default,* IMF Working Paper, International Monetary Fund, 2008, available at: https://www.imf.org/en/Publications/WP/Issues/2016/12/31/The-Costs-of-Sovereign-Default-22346

Brewer Carías, Allan R., "Public Power" in *Political and Constitutional Institutions,* Volume II, Caracas, pp 144.

Brewer-Carías, Allan R., "The vicissitudes of the payment of the external private debt and the legal incongruities of the executive power" in *Revista de Derecho Público,* N° 27, Editorial Jurídica Venezolana, Caracas, 1986, pp 36-49.

Brewer-Carías, Allan R., "New considerations on the legal regime of State contracts in Venezuela" in *Revista de Derecho Administrativo,* No. 2, Caracas, 2006, available at: https://revistas.pucp.edu.pe/index.php/derechoadministrativo/article/view/16331

Brewer-Carías, Allan R., "The National Assembly's failed attempt to exercise political control over the public administration by investigating PDVSA's actions, and its annulment by the Constitutional Chamber" in *Revista de Derecho Público,* No. 147-148, Editorial Jurídica Venezolana, Caracas, 2016, p. 359, available at: https://revistadederechopublico.com/archivos/articulos/el-intento-fallido-de-la-asamblea-nacional-de-ejercer-el-control-politico-sobre-la-administracion-publica-investigando-la-actuacion-de-pdvsa-y-su-anulacion-por-la-sala-constitucional

Brewer-Carías, Allan R., "Judicial disregard of the power of the National Assembly to legislate", in *Revista de Derecho Público,* No. 145-146, Editorial Jurídica Venezolana, Caracas, 2016, pp 377-426.

Buchheit, Lee, and Gulati, Mitu, "How to Restructure Greek Debt", in *Duke Law School Public Law & Legal Theory Series,* May 2010, available at: http://dx.doi.org/10.2139/ssrn.1603304

Buchheit, Lee, and Gulati, Mitu, "How to Restructure Venezuelan Debt", in *Duke Law School Public Law & Legal Theory Series,* No. 52, August 2017, available at: https://scholarship.law.duke.edu/faculty_scholarship/3758

Calvo, Guillermo, "Servicing the Public Debt: The Role of Expectations", in *The American Economic Review,* Vol. 78, No. 4 (Sep), 1988, pp 647-661.

Carrasquero, Andrés, Escovar, Ramón, and Campos, Mariana, *Venezuelan External Debt Derived from Bonds,* Public Spending Observatory, CEDICE Libertad, Caracas, 2022, available at: https://cedice.org.ve/ogp/reporte/deuda-externa-venezolana-derivada-de-los-bonos/

Carrasquero, Andrés, Escovar, Ramón, and Campos, Mariana, *The Restructuring of Venezuelan External Debt: Experiences, Limits and Effective Proposals,* CEDICE Libertad, Caracas, 2022, available at: https://cedice.org.ve/ogp/wp-content/uploads/2022/12/Reestructuracion-deuda-ext.-venezolana-3.pdf

Carrasquero, Andrés, Escovar, Ramón, Campos, Mariana, and Freitas, Víctor, *Sovereign debt restructuring processes: lessons learned for Venezuela from Uruguay, Greece, Puerto Rico and Argentina,* CEDICE Libertad, Caracas, 2023, p. 6, available at: https://cedice.org.ve/ogp/wp-content/uploads/2023/08/Reestructuracion-Deuda-OGP.pdf

Clarke, Ben, "Agrokor granted Chapter 15 protection in New York", in *Global Restructuring Review,* 24/09/2018, available at: https://globalrestructuringreview.com/article/agrokor-granted-chapter-15-protection-in-new-york

Comín, Francisco, *The sovereign debt crises in Spain (1500-2015),* Ed. Los Libros de la Catarata, Madrid, 2016.

Das, Udaibir, Papaioannou, Michael G., and Trebesch, Christoph, *Sovereign Debt Restructurings 1950-2010: Concepts, Literature Survey, and Stylized Facts,* IMF Working Paper WP/12/203, International Monetary Fund, Washington, 2012, available at: https://www.imf.org/en/Publications/WP/Issues/2016/12/31/Sovereign-Debt-Restructurings-1950-2010-Literature-Survey-Data-and-Stylized-Facts-26190

United States Department of the Treasury, "The History of the Debt", on *TreasuryDirect,* available at: https://treasurydirect.gov/government/historical-debt-outstanding/

Dialogue Earth, "China is a long-term player in Venezuela's energy future", available at: https://dialogue.earth/en/energy/6895-china-is-a-long-term-player-in-venezuelas-energy-future/

Dippelsman, Robert, Dziobek, Claudia and Gutiérrez Mangas, Carlos, *What Lies Beneath: The Statistical Definition of Public Sector Debt,* IMF Staff Discussion Note, International Monetary Fund, Washington, 2012, available at: https://www.imf.org/external/pubs/ft/sdn/2012/sdn1209.pdf

Duque Corredor, Román, "Nullity of PDVSA 2020 Bonds" in *Revista de Derecho Público,* No. 161-162, Editorial Jurídica Venezolana, Caracas, 2022, pp 349-352, available at: https://revistadederechopublico.com/wp-content/uploads/2022/12/Revista-de-Derecho-Publico-No-161-162-2020-cov.-txt-4-1-2.pdf

Easterly, William, "Debt Relief," in *Foreign Policy,* Vol. 127, Nov/Dec. 2001, pp 20-26.

Easterly, William, "How Did Heavily Indebted Poor Countries Become Heavily Indebted? Reviewing Two Decades of Debt Relief", Policy Research Working Paper, in *World Development,* Vol. 30-10, 2022, available at: https://documents.worldbank.org/en/publication/documents-reports/documentdetail/232501468739141596/how-did-highly-indebted-poor-countries-become-highly-indebted-reviewing-two-decades-of-debt-relief

Edwards, Sebastian, *Capital Flows, Foreign Direct Investment and Debt-equity swaps in developing countries,* National Bureau of Economic Research, 1990.

Escobar, Gustavo, "The Labyrinth of Economics" in Naím, Moisés, and Piñango, Ramón, *The Case of Venezuela: an illusion of harmony,* IESA, Caracas, 1985, pp 71-101.

Expansión, "Argentine Public Debt – 2022", on *Datosmacro.com,* available at: www.datosmacro.expansion.com/deuda/Argentina

Expansion, "Greek Public Debt – 2011", on *Datosmacro.com,* available at: www.datosmacro.expansion.com/deuda/Grecia

Fabela, Isidro, *The Monroe and Drago Doctrines,* National Autonomous University of Mexico, Mexico City, 1957.

Ferrer, Elías, *"Venezuela's long and winding debt restructuring road"* in *Financial Times,* Vol. March 2019, available at: https://www.ft.com/content/629ba3b7-2e4b-49d7-9d00-e70e7cb4f3af

International Monetary Fund / International Monetary Fund, *External Debt Statistics: Guide for Compilers and Users,* Washington, 2023, available at: https://www.imf.org/external/pubs/ft/eds/Eng/Guide/index.htm

International Monetary Fund / International Monetary Fund, *World Economic Outlook - 2020,* Washington, 2020.

Forte, Santiago, and Peña, Juan, "Debt refinancing and credit risk", in *Spanish Review of Financial Economics (Revista de Economía Financiera),* Vol. 9-1, Madrid, July, 2010, available at: https://papers.ssrn.com/sol3/papers.cfm?abstract_id=1689903

Ganitsky, Joseph; and Lema, Gerardo; "Foreign Investment Through Debt-Equity Swaps," in *MIT Sloan Management Review,* Cambridge Vol. 29(2), Winter 1998.

Graeber, David, *Debt: The First 5000 Years,* Melville House Publishing, New York, 2011.

Grosse, Robert, "The Debt/Equity Swap in Latin America- In Whose Interest?" in *Journal of International Financial Management and Accounting,* Vol. 4(1), March 1992

Guzmán, Martín and Stiglitz, Joseph, *A "Soft Law" Mechanism for Sovereign Debt Restructuring. Based on the UN Principles,* Friedrich Ebert Stiftung, New York, 2016, available at: https://library.fes.de/pdf-files/iez/13425.pdf

Hernández Delfino, Carlos, "The Baker Plan for Debt: Outline for an Evaluation", *Prodavinci,* Caracas, 2021, available at: https://prodavinci.com/el-plan-baker-para-la-deuda-bosquejo-para-una-evaluacion/

Hernández Delfino, Carlos, "Venezuela and the Brady Initiative", *Prodavinci,* Caracas, 2021, available at: https://prodavinci.com/venezuela-y-la-iniciativa-brady/

Hernández, José Ignacio, "What is happening with Venezuela's external public debt?", in *La Gran Aldea,* Caracas, Feb. 2022.

Hernández, José Ignacio, "Regarding the PDVSA 2020 bond case and the interapplication of commercial and constitutional law", in *Revista Venezolana de Derecho Mercantil,* No. 6, 2021, Caracas, pp. 105-133, available at: http://www.ulpiano.org.ve/revistas/bases/artic/texto/RVDM/6/RVDM_2021_6_105-133.pdf

Hernández, José Ignacio, *The Venezuelan External Public Debt Crisis: Everything Everywhere All at Once,* Center for Strategic and International Studies, Washington, 2023, available at: https://www.csis.org/analysis/venezuelan-external-public-debt-crisis-everything-everywhere-all-once

Hinrichsen, Simon, "The Iraq sovereign debt restructuring", in *Capital Markets Law Journal,* Vol. 16 (1), January 2021.

Humes, Hans, "Thoughts *on the Possible Restructuring of Venezuelan Debt"* (interview*)*, LEC Abogados, Caracas, 2023, available at: https://www.lec.com.ve/en/home/#blog

Independent Evaluation Group, *Debt Relief for the Poorest. An Evaluation Update of the HIPC Initiative,* World Bank/World Bank, Washington, 2006, available at: https://openknowledge.worldbank.org/server/api/core/bitstreams/bb514953-7881-52ba-a0f3-948412a47d1c/content

Italiani, Fulvio, Omaña, Carlos and Pettersson, Roland, "Refinancing Venezuela's Debt: Local Legal and Policy Issues" in *The Guide to Restructuring - 3rd* [Ed]., LatinLawyer, Jun-2024, available at: https://latinlawyer.com/guide/the-guide-restructuring/third-edition/article/refinancing-venezuelas-debt-local-legal-and-policy-issues

Karanasos, Menelaos, Koutroumpis, Panagiotis, Hatgioannides, John, *et al.,* "The Greek Drachma: 5 Years of Austerity. The Three Economists' View and a Comment" in *Papers on Greece and Southeast Europe,* No. 113, Hellenic Observatory of the London School of Economics, London, August 2017, available at: https://www.lse.ac.uk/Hellenic-Observatory/Assets/Documents/Publications/GreeSE-Papers/GreeSE-No113.pdf

Kargman, Steven, "Venezuela's Potential Debt Restructuring and Economic Recovery Efforts: Some Key Legal and Policy Challenges" in *Revista Venezolana de Legislación y Jurisprudencia,* No. 13, Caracas, 2020, pp. 163-190, available at: https://hlsbankruptcyr.wpengine.com/wp-content/uploads/2020/07/RVLJ-13-163-190_S.Kargman_Venezuela_Debt_Restructuring_and_Economic_Recovery_FINAL.pdf

Kargman, Steven, "Venezuela: Prospects for Restructuring Sovereign Debt and Rebuilding a National Economy against the backdrop of a Failing State", in Journal of the *Association of Insolvency & Restructuring Advisors (AIRA),* 2021, available at: https://blogs.law.ox.ac.uk/business-law-blog/blog/2021/10/venezuela-prospects-restructuring-sovereign-debt-and-rebuilding

Kargman, Steven, "Thoughts *on the Possible Restructuring of Venezuelan Debt"* (interview*)*, LEC Abogados, Caracas, 2023, available at: https://www.lec.com.ve/en/home/#blog

Katsikas, Dimitris, "The Greek economic crisis of 2012" in *CIDOB International Yearbook 2013,* p. 197 et seq., available at: https://www.raco.cat/index.php/AnuarioCIDOB

Kelly, Janet, "State-owned enterprises. From commonplace to common sense" in Naím, Moisés, and Piñango, Ramón, *The Case of Venezuela: an illusion of harmony,* IESA, Caracas, 1985, p. 141.

Kotze, Antonie, "Debt, Defaults and Crises: A Historical Perspective" (working paper), Financial Chaos Theory Pty. Ltd., 2015.

Krueger, Anne, *A New Approach To Sovereign Debt Restructuring,* International Monetary Fund, Washington, 2002.

Laryea, Thomas, *Approaches to Corporate Debt Restructuring in the Wake of Financial Crises,* IMF Staff Position Note, International Monetary Fund, Washington, 2010, available at: https://www.imf.org/external/pubs/ft/spn/2010/spn1002.pdf

LEC Abogados, "Thoughts on the Possible Restructuring of Venezuelan Debt" (interview *(series)*, Caracas, 2023, available at: https://www.lec.com.ve/en/home/#blog

Levin, Richard, and Pettersson, Roland, "A New PDVSA? The Transfer of Venezuela's Oil Assets to a Successor Entity and Fraudulent Conveyance", in *Capital Markets Law Journal,* Vol. March-19, Oxford University Press, 2019, available at: https://papers.ssrn.com/sol3/papers.cfm?abstract_id=3349158

Liehr, Reinhard, "The external debt of Gran Colombia to Great Britain 1820-1860" in *The public debt in Latin America in historical perspective,* Biblioteca Ibero-Americana Vervuert, Madrid, 1995, pp 466-488, available at: https://publications.iai.spk-berlin.de/receive/riai_mods_00002381

Looney, Robert, "Venezuela's Economic Crisis: Origins and Successes in Stabilization", in *Journal of Social, Political and Economic Studies,* Council for Social and Economic Studies, 1986, pp 327-337.

Lowenthal, Abraham F., *Venezuela's Elusive Transition: Toward a New Path,* Wilson Center, Washington, 2021, available at: https://www.wilsoncenter.org/publication/venezuelas-elusive-transition-toward-new-path

Marichal, Carlos, *History of Latin America's External Debt: From Independence to the Great Depression, 1820-1930,* Alianza Editorial, Mexico City, 1988, pp 17 et seq.

Maza Zavala, Domingo, "Debt 1935-1993" in *Dictionary of Venezuelan History,* Volume 2, Fundación Empresas Polar, 2nd Ed., Caracas, 2011, p. 95.

McCoy, Jennifer, "The Politics of Adjustment: Labor and the Venezuelan Debt Crisis" in *Journal of Interamerican Studies and World Affairs,* V. 28-4, Cambridge University Press, 1987, p. 103.

Milevsky, Moshe, *The Day the King Defaulted: Financial Lessons from the Stop of the Exchequer in 1672,* Macmillan, 2017.

Mitchell, Nancy, "Venezuela Blockade (1902–1903)" in Martel, Gordon, *The Encyclopedia of War,* Wiley-Blackwell, London, 2011.

Moatti, Thomas, and Muci, Frank, *An Economic Framework for Venezuela's Debt Restructuring,* Harvard Kennedy School, Boston, 2019, available at: https://www.hks.harvard.edu/sites/default/files/degree%20programs/MPAID/files/Moatti%2C%20Thomas%20and%20Muci%2C%20Frank%20SYPA.pdf

Moreno, María Antonia, "The Organic Law of Financial Administration of the Public Sector. Content, scope and limitations" in *Venezuelan Journal of Current Analysis,* Vol. VII-2, Central University of Venezuela, Caracas, 2001.

Morgan Stanley, "Investors Evaluate Developments in Venezuela," in *MS Insights,* January 2026, available at: https://www.morganstanley.com/insights/articles/market-implications-us-intervention-venezuela

Ocampo, José Antonio, "The Urgency of Sovereign-Debt Restructuring" (April 18, 2024), in *Project Syndicate,* New York, 2024, available at: https://www.project-syndicate.org/commentary/world-needs-comprehensive-debt-restructuring-mechanism-by-jose-antonio-ocampo-2024-04

Olivares-Caminal, Rodrigo, "Thoughts *on the Possible Restructuring of Venezuelan Debt"* (interview), LEC Abogados, Caracas, 2023, available at: https://www.lec.com.ve/en/home/#blog

Oría, Salvador, *Finance,* Ed. Kraft, Buenos Aires, 1948.

Pargas Mujica, Luis, "Analysis of Venezuelan public debt during the period 1999-2019" in *Revista Alternativas of the Catholic University of Santiago de Guayaquil,* Vol. 20-1, Ecuador, 2019, available at: https://dialnet.unirioja.es/servlet/articulo?codigo=7445920

Paris, María, "Is Venezuela Headed to Debt Restructuring?", *Caracas Chronicles,* May 2024, available at: https://www.caracaschronicles.com/2024/05/06/is-venezuela-headed-to-debt-restructuring/

Pellegrino, Cosimina and Louza, Laura, "PDVSA signed a contract of national public interest without even the endorsement of the National Assembly" in *Revista de Derecho Público,* No. 171-172, Editorial Jurídica Venezolana, Caracas, 2022, p. 111, available at: https://revistadederechopublico.com/archivos/revistas/revista-de-derecho-publico-director-no-171-172-julio-diciembre-2022

Pimentel y Roth, Francisco, *History of public credit in Venezuela,* Ed. Ministry of Public Credit, Caracas, 1974.

Pimentel y Roth, Francisco, *History of public credit in Venezuela,* General Archive of the Nation, 1974.

Pimentel, Francisco, *Chronological summary of the laws and decrees of public credit in Venezuela since the year 1826,* Ed. Ministry of Public Credit, Caracas, 1873.

Portes, Richard, Freixas, Xavier, Dewatripont, Mathías, *Macroeconomic Stability and Financial Regulation,* Center for Economic and Policy Research, London, 2009, available at: https://cepr.org/system/files/publication-files/68581-macroeconomic_stability_and_financial_regulation_key_issues_for_the_g20.pdf

Rancic, Nedad, "Agrokor. A case of controlled collapse", in Beros, Recker *et al., Economic and Social Development: 27th International Scientific Conference on Economic and Social Development,* Croatia, 2018, pp 753-762.

Reinhart, Carmen; Rogoff, Kenneth; Savastano, Miguel, "Debt Intolerance" in *Brookings Papers on Economic Activity,* Vol. 1, 1-74, 2003.

Rengel Núñez, Pedro, "The notorious case of the PDVSA 2020 bonds", in *Revista Venezolana de Derecho Mercantil,* No. 5, Caracas, 2020, pp. 35-58, available at: https://www.traviesoevans.com/travieso/el-sonado-caso-de-los-bonos-pdvsa-2020-pedro-rengel-nunez/

Rodríguez, Francisco, *Sanctions, Economic Statecraft, and Venezuela's Crisis - Case Study,* Sanctions and Security Research Project, Ed. Fourth Freedom Forum, 2022, p. 8, available at: https://sanctionsandsecurity.org/publications/sanctions-economic-statecraft-and-venezuelas-crisis/

Rodríguez, Francisco, "Can Venezuela Chart a Path Out of Crisis?", in *Foreign Affairs,* Vol. Dec, 2023, available at: https://www.foreignaffairs.com/united-states/can-venezuela-chart-path-out-crisis

Rodríguez Campos, Manuel, "Internal debt and external debt (1810-1930)" in *Dictionary of Venezuelan History,* Volume 2, Fundación Empresas Polar, 2nd Ed., Caracas, 2011.

Rojas Sardi, Armando, *The United States and the 1902 blockade: external debt: aggression of the new times,* Ed. National Academy of History, Caracas, 1992.

Sachs, Jeffrey, *The End of Poverty: Economic Possibilities for Our Time,* Penguin Press, New York, 2005.

Salazar, Andrés, and Ospina, Ramón, "The blockade of the Venezuelan coast: a brief clash with European imperialism" in *Scientific Journal,* 9(31), 68-86, 2024, available at: https://www.indteca.com/ojs/index.php/Revista_Scientific/article/view/944

Sansó, Beatrice, "Jurisdictional immunity in Article 151 of the 1999 Constitution", in *Homage Book to Enrique Tejera París, Topics on the 1999 Constitution,* Center for Legal Research, Caracas, 2001, p. 333-368.

Santos, Miguel, "Venezuela: Anatomy of a Collapse and a Roadmap for Reconstruction", presentation at the forum *The Venezuela That Is Coming. Political and Economic Solutions,* Andrés Bello University, Santiago, Chile, 2019, available at: https://www.slideshare.net/slideshow/venezuela-anatoma-de-un-colapso-y-una-hoja-de-ruta-para-la-reconstruccin/138471758

Seelke R., Clare, "Venezuela: Overview of US Sanctions Policy", US Congressional Research Service (CRS), Washington, 202 0 (updated 2024), available at: https://crsreports.congress.gov/product/pdf/IF/IF10715

Sturzenegger, Federico; Zettelmeyer, Jeromin, "Haircuts: Estimating investor losses in sovereign debt restructurings, 1998–2005, in *Journal of International Money and Finance,* Vol. 27(5), September 2008.

Tamburini, Francesco, "History and destiny of the "Calvo Doctrine": current relevance or obsolescence of Carlos Calvo's thought?" in *Journal of Historical-Legal Studies,* International Law, Valparaíso, Chile, 2002, available at: https://www.scielo.cl/scielo.php?script=sci_arttext&pid=S0716-54552002002400005

Taylor, Adam, "How Citgo, a US oil company, became Venezuela's lifeline" (01/29/2019), in *The Washington Post,* available at: https://www.washingtonpost.com/world/2019/01/29/how-citgo-us-oil-company-became-venezuelas-lifeline/

Toro Jiménez, Fermín, *Manual of Public International Law,* Caracas, 1982, pp. 481 et seq.

Vera, Leonardo, "The external public debt that destroyed a country, leaps once again into the arena" in *PolitikaUcab - Journal of the Center for Political and Government Studies,* Andrés Bello Catholic University, Caracas, 2020, available at: https://politikaucab.net/2020/09/22/la-deuda-publica-externa-que-acabo-con-un-pais-salta-una-vez-mas-al-ruedo/

Walker, Mark, "Thoughts *on the Possible Restructuring of Venezuelan Debt"* (interview*)*, LEC Abogados, Caracas, 2023, available at: https://www.lec.com.ve/en/home/#blog

Walker, Mark, and Cooper, Richard, "Venezuela's Restructuring: A Path Forward" in *Emerging Markets Restructuring Journal,* Cleary Gottlieb, Summer 2019, available at: https://www.clearygottlieb.com/-/media/files/emrj-materials/issue-9-2018/venezuelas-restructuring--a-path-forward-pdf.pdf

Wallenstein, Stephen, "Debt-Equity Swaps and Conversion Funds" (Chapter 6), in Effros, Robert, *Current Legal Issues Affecting Central Banks,* Vol. II, Ed. International Monetary Fund, 1994, available at: https://www.elibrary.imf.org/configurable/content/book$002f9781557753069$002fch006.xml?t:ac=book%24002f9781557753069%24002fch006.xml

Weisbrot, Mark and Johnston, Jake, *Venezuela's Economic Recovery: Is it Sustainable?,* Center for Economic and Policy Research, London, 2012, available at: https://cepr.net/publications/venezuelas-economic-recovery-is-it-sustainable/

World Bank, *Global Financial Development Database,* Washington, available at: https://www.worldbank.org/en/publication/gfdr/data/global-financial-development-database

Yapur, Nicolle, "Venezuela, in default, hires Rothschild as debt advisor" (April 23, 2024), in *Bloomberg (Bloomberg Line),* available at: https://www.bloomberglinea.com/latinoamerica/venezuela/venezuela-en-default-contrata-a-rothschild-como-asesor-de-deuda/

Youkee, Mat, "Venezuela Sovereign Debt: A Hefty Wager", in *LatinFinance,* Q3-2023, available at: https://latinfinance.com/magazine/2023-q3/2023/07/24/venezuela-sovereign-debt-a-hefty-wager/

Zandstra, Deborah, "Thoughts *on the Possible Restructuring of Venezuelan Debt"* (interview*)*, LEC Abogados, Caracas, 2023, available at: https://www.lec.com.ve/en/home/#blog

www.ingramcontent.com/pod-product-compliance
Lightning Source LLC
Chambersburg PA
CBHW031330230926
51848CB00001B/171
* 9 7 8 9 8 0 1 8 7 9 4 4 2 *